HASHMAKERS

(Grandpa Windsong's Tales From The 60's)

Ark Press
PO Box 584
Woodstock, NY
12498
ISBN: 978-1-939374-02-8
Copyright 2013
E-Mail Acousticman1@hotmail.com
Facebook: Peter Walker

INDEX

INTRODUCTION

In Cambridge Mass in 1963 during the JFK Administration there was a thriving colony of intellectuals, folksingers, genius instrumentalists, brilliant professors kids with "off the chart" IQ's", and a surprising number of bi-coastal young people who "lived by their wits". They lived in inexpensive student market housing. Some were from wealthy families and who were able to afford their Shelby Cobra sports cars, rare Martin guitars, and high-end drugs. Others had dropped out or were alienated from their parents and were living "underground." Many were talented artist's, others brilliant researchers or musicians, others were just good at surviving and networking.

It was all relatively harmless. The local Cambridge City police, "lowest paid police force in the country," preferred the Status Quo. A little pot smoking was quite tolerable to them as long as it didn't spread into the student dorms. They reserved their awesome wrath and police brutality for the occasional idiot that tried to market any kind of "hard drugs" (amphetamine or heroin) to their beloved (huge economic resource) students. Actually the MIT and Harvard University Campus Police were well paid and effective. Any drug use was strictly on the fringes. There were however fringe communities who were curious, about what drugs were and what they could do and were active in their defense of their right to experiment. They called themselves "The International Foundation for Internal Freedom". Using much of the rhetoric that would ultimately persuade the Supreme Court of the US in Roe V Wade. They proclaimed a Declaration of Internal Chemical Freedom. "A person is sovereign over their own body and it's chemistry". Conspicuous proponents included Dr. Timothy Leary, and Dr. Richard Alpert (Baba Ram Das).

Others individuals in this social rubric had nothing to do with drugs. They were in hot pursuit of excellence in their chosen area of interest. Electronics whiz kids, exotic instrumentalists, folkloric minutia collectors, some blues fans made a point of learning every riff from every blues record ever published. Among the bluegrass fans later to be famous Bill Kieth could pick faster than Earl Scruggs. A young man called Don West was the greatest "Travis picker" that anyone had ever seen or heard of. A 17-year-old young black classical guitarist from the worst neighborhood in Boston blew everyone away. Bull sessions went long into the nights with world class music and flashing wits.

Many Famous names in The Folk Music World emerged out of the Cambridge subculture of that era. Joan Baez, Jimmy Kweskin and the Jug Band, Eric Von Schmidt, The Charles River Valley Boys, Tim Hardin, Karen Dalton and Taj Majal, to name just a few. They were all part of a community that had a tradition of "pursuit of excellence". They all had peer "permission" to be the best in the world at their chosen endeavors.

This is a story about two of these people.

One was a young, extraordinarily beautiful, brilliant, talented very upscale young NYC woman who was trying to escape from the obsessive control of her wealthy parents. Her father was enamored of her in a borderline inappropriate way. It wasn't that he didn't love her, on the contrary, he was worried about her in a rather normal way for the father of a beautiful young woman, who was realizing that she she had wings, and wanted to fly.

It was why she had come to Boston to finish her graduate degree. The father visited often and offered rewards and incentives if she would only return to NY. For her part she wanted to see the world and was afraid of being "boxed in" to a confined life. She knew her father had detectives watching her, she had found bills marked "Bonded Detective Agency" in her fathers desk on a visit home.

She was aware that she was more attractive and smarter than all of her peers but was unaware of quite how extraordinary she was. Like most young people she was attracted to what was considered "cool" or "hip". The difference in her case is that she was on the cutting edge of finding out just what that was.

The other was a young man who had far more real world experience then others his age. Possessed of plenty of intuitive "street smarts" he was a veteran traveler. He was a talented player of many instruments, a successful local businessman and a voracious reader with a really high IQ. His peers held him in high esteem and he possessed a passionate social conscience. As a result of his activism on behalf of children and civil rights he had come to the favorable attention of the younger Kennedy brothers. Even the local Mob was amused and impressed by his ability to freely import and smoke right under the government's noses. At that time in that scene and setting he was what was "cool & hip", or at least he was on the cutting edge of whatever that was.

PROLOGUE

Paco's father had raised him to be a "Gudjefian Minimalist" with aspirations of being an "Entrepreneurial Capitalist" (sans capital). His Father in a very real sense had "lived by his wits".

In 1944 when Paco was 6 years old with Christmas around the corner and money very tight, his father had set out with the big old bellows camera and tripod that he kept in the basement and had returned a few days later with wads of money in every pocket. Apparently while school pictures were regularly taken in the grammar and high schools no one had photographed and sold prints to the parents of the various kindergarten students around Boston until that week. He had taken pictures of all the classes, written the name of the school and the year on the bottom of the negative in white ink, and then printed as many prints as there were students. They had

nearly all paid a dollar each for a copy of the "class picture".
It was a great Christmas.

As an eight-year-old the young man had been with his father
one afternoon when his fathers car ran low on gas in the
middle of Boston. Calling his father's attention to the low gas
gauge and pointing out that he and his brother were hungry he
watched his dad look in his wallet and find it empty. What
Paco would never forget was what his father did next.

Pulling over to the curb his father went to the trunk of the car
and reaching into a cardboard carton that was always kept
there he returned with a large bundle of ball point pens, a shoe
box top, a piece of sandpaper and a handful of rubber bands.
Working quickly his father had repeatedly filled the shoe box
top with the pens, scratched the barrels of the entire shoe box
top with a fast pass of the sandpaper, then with what was
obviously a practiced motion he scooped the pens up into
bundles of ten. Slipping a rubber band over each of the
bundles he stuffed the pockets of his suit coat until it bulged
all over. Taking a single last pen a small pad of paper from

the dashboard he exited the car and disappeared into an office building across the street.

 A few minutes later he emerged with no bulges in his pockets and a fistful of dollars in his hand. His father reentered the car, gave some money to Paco's brother to get sandwiches and soda, and pulled into the corner gas station. The entire process had taken less than fifteen minutes. Paco said "Dad, what did you just do?" "Sold some pens" his father said. "How much did you sell them for?" "Ten for a dollar" was the response. "Well, how much did they cost you?" " Three and a half cents each". "But Dad, that's a 300 percent profit" Paco was incredulous. "I know", said his father, who had paid for his gas and was stuffing the rest of the money into his wallet. With them all contentedly having lunch they had continued on their way.

 Paco had one more question. "Why did you scratch them with the sand paper?" His father replied "so they would be factory seconds. No one would buy them if they were brand new and ten for a dollar, there had to be a reason why they

were so cheap. I created that reason when I scratched them",
he explained. "Look" he said, demonstrating his "sales
pitch," "Perfectly good pens, factory seconds, see the scratch?
But they write perfectly well" and he would demonstrate on
the little pad of paper. " Ten for a dollar". Because offices
always needed pens they always went for it and it only took a
few minutes to sell out. It was Paco's first experience with
the profit potential of insights into other people's psychology.

Paco's mother had a different agenda for Paco. She was a
Music Conservatory graduate and had gegun a successful
career as a concert pianist. A soloist with the 1st all woman's
orchestra in the US, she had broken off her career to marry
Paco's father but was determined that the family was going to
produce a great pianist. She wanted him to be it.

She had about as much chance of achieving that goal as a pig
had flying. 1st of all he escaped practice at every single
opportunity, 2nd His interest was in his fathers guitar and
mandolin not his mothers Mozart. Nevertheless he was forced
to turn pages two afternoons a week as his mother and her

former professor from the conservatory thundered through four-handed Mozart in an effort to try and interest him. After four years of failed attempts she gave up. After trying his father's mandolin Paco settled on the guitar and wore the strings out. After that he mastered the harmonica.

Unlike other kids he knew in Boston he had grown up (in the spring summer and fall) in a large mansion on Cape Cod with a private beach and a large library of Medical and Classical literature. The story was that his father had listened sympathetically to the elderly owner complain that she couldn't keep up the estate and mansion "the way he used to" and lived in another house on the property. Paco had been amazed to find out that his father paid 100 dollars a year for the lease on the house he grown up in on the "condition that he kept up the house like the old Dr. would have". The lease was good "for the life of the building". It was a lot of work but had many benefits. They had a small skiff aptly dubbed "the sieve". They would make different sail plans for it (gaff, marconi, and lateen) and sail around the nearby islands and adjacent harbors, bailing constantly. There were ten acres of woods out back leading to a Marsh at the end of a harbor to roam in. Paco knew kids with more things but no one with so much space.

The harbor was used for shell fishing, and one day Paco noticed that all the professional shell fisherman were limited in how far they could go out at low tide by the height of their "hip boots". He got swim fins and a mask and tried diving out past where anyone had shellfished before going into deeper water. He hit paydirt. There were lots of large shellfish easily harvestable. To stay under water longer Paco grabbed the bellows from the fireplace, and screwed it to the front of the skiff. Putting a bedspring between the handles of the bellows to keep it open he attached a string to the top handle with a counter weight on the bottom. When the string was pulled from underwater, it would pull the bellows shut and force air through a hose attached to the nozzle. The bedspring would reopen the bellows and the process could be repeated with another tug on the string. Anchored in maybe 10 feet of water Paco was able to stay down for 20 minutes at a time. He harvested many buckets full, which he sold to neighborhood housewives to make chowder with for a dollar a bucketful.

Another entrepreneurial endeavor was the fireworks. Fireworks were illegal in Mass, but could be bought in far away Connecticut. By planning for the following year ahead of time Paco would beg, cajole, entreat and bribe regular summer visitors from N.Y. and Connecticut into stopping and "picking him up some fireworks so he could celebrate the 4th of July". Some did. Paco did a brisk trade with the other kids. Ten-cent packs of ladyfingers went for a dollar and 5-cent cherry bombs were 25cents each. At times the peaceful beach community sounded like a war zone. His father tolerated this activity with a benevolent pride. "Boys will be boys" he would say when his mother fretted about "blowing his fingers off".

Late one night when the house was full of guests and they were all settled in for the evening in the living room a very loud explosion rocked the porch just out side the window.

Paco was blamed. He tried to prove that it couldn't have been his. He even gathered the remnants of the "3 inch salute" that had done the deed and deduced that it had been carefully wedged in. between two boards on the porch to increase its explosive energy. One of the boards had been blown loose. He did everything he could think of to try and prove his case. "Nope" his father said if "it wasn't you then it was someone you supplied." His "stock in trade" of fireworks was confiscated, dunked in water, and forbidden henceforth. He never did find out who did it, and was grounded for the rest of the season.

It wasn't so bad. He spent many happy hours in the 18th century Doctors library of the old Mansion with the Franklin stove burning and reading material unavailable anywhere else at the time. Two books really impressed him. There were first editions of "Confession's of an English Opium Eater" and "Confessions of a Hashish Eater." He read lithographed old volumes of Dickens, and Shakespeare (his father's favorite). His father's other favorite was Goethe but Paco wasn't ready for that yet. He discovered Terhune and Penrod.

He preferred History and anything else he could get his hands on that had a story or an adventure attached to it. He especially liked the Dickens.

The problem was for Paco, that no one talked that way anymore. When he attempted to speak in Classical English to his teachers and peers they just looked at him strangely. Paco's Mother had objected, "you should be outside" she said and to his father she said. "He's not normal."

Paco's father encouraged this reading obsession. Later when Paco lived on his own, about once a week he would open the door to his apartment and find a waist high stack of books. He would know that his father had been there in the early morning and had left them. They had been lovingly picked out at the various stalls and used book stores which his Dad habitually haunted. Travel, classics, humor, adventure, chess strategy, especially history. Anything that his father thought would broaden his son's mental horizons. Paco would smile and shake his head and then usually read most of each stack.

One of the reasons for the "economic ups and downs" of Paco's childhood was his father's social habits. Always in possession of a "speed graphic" professional "press" camera Paco was amazed when his father took him to a Red Socks Game and instead of buying a ticket he would tuck a card into his hatband and walk past the ticket collector lifting the camera and saying "press". It always worked. Most evenings his dad was gone. For years during the winter months his father had been employed at a small salary as the manager of a small hotel located next to Boston's City Hall. This had brought him into contact with then Mayor Curley.

Mayor Curley was best known around Boston for stealing every cent he could from every state and federal and county program. His enemies were overjoyed when, a few days before an election, the Mayor was caught with his hand in the cookie jar, arrested and thrown into Charles Street Jail.

On the eve of the election, a team of auditors reported that yes the Mayor had in fact stolen all that money and much, much, more. This made his enemies rejoice. It was also found that he had spent every cent on building parks in the poorest neighborhoods, providing fuel in the cold Boston winters for the elderly, bought books to raise the standards of the schools, and established a medical care system that treated all poor Bostonians without cost. The opposition was crushed.

 He was reelected by a landslide and because there was a law at the time that an elected Mayor could not be incarcerated on his way to his own swearing in, he was released and driven in a police car back to City Hall.

For Paco it was a great sociopolitical lesson for young man in his formative years.

With his ubiquitous Speed Graphic, Paco's father became the unofficial photographer of the Curley administration. Taking photos of the Mayor with various visiting fireman and dignitaries at "Lockovers", he would be gone until the wee hours.

Paco's mom objected when Paco's Pop told the story about how during Prohibition his grandfather had owned a yawl and had announced to his neighbors the he was "off to Florida". Sailing down the inland waterway to Florida his grandfather had stayed a few days and then announced "I'm off to Bimini". Making a dead run for Jamaica his Grandfather had loaded the Yawl awash with rum, made a straight run towards the north Atlantic, and one foggy night guided by the bells he had brought the ship into a secluded cove in Maine. After unloading, he sold the rum and bought a big old house. Paco treasured pictures of the house and regarded the old photos as proof of the truth of the tale.

"That's not normal" his mother said.

When he was 11, his mother had left his father for a steadily employed member of the "establishment". His mother won custody of the two sons. This was traumatic on several levels. Besides the obvious separation anxiety, he would miss his dad's guitar and mandolin playing. With his fathers encouragement he had established a paper collection system that employed other kids who collected and bundled old newspaper. Paco resold them in half-ton lots to jobbers and was making about 12 dollars a week selling wholesale waste paper. A princely sum for an 11-year-old in 1949. Moving meant no more income. Also Paco had been engaged in regular Saturday trading sessions with his peers which had, over a period of some months, netted him an extensive collection of rare cap-guns 1st edition comic books, various military surplus items, and a real pinball machine.

When the time came to leave their fathers house, in a misguided effort to sever the children's memories, each child was allowed to take only one toy from his "old life" on to the "new life" his mother had designed for them. "Your going to lead a normal life now, dear", his mother had said.

He was forbidden to see his father. He was not allowed any books.

For the next year to his surprise, no one supervised Paco. His mother was gone to her new spouse's house waiting out the

Massachusetts one-year divorce decree waiting period. Paco had been essentially "parked" at his Godmothers house who was also gone working two jobs at the time. His brother, who to his great credit, had objected to his mothers decision, was gone working at a fantastic opportunity job arranged by the new husband to be in an effort to shut him up and cooperate with the divorce and remarriage process. His brother took the job but didn't change his opinion. The hostility was palpable.

The Godmother left out meals, but no one was ever home. He got himself to school but later would never remember going. He was given a dollar a week and permission to go the movies at night by himself. To all intents and purposes he was emancipated. Because he had once witnessed a sexual assault in a movie theater and because he felt he had good reason to be afraid of bigger kids and teenagers, Paco started to carry a knife. He also went to the used paperback bookstores. At 15 cents a book he funded his reading by finding and cashing in soda bottles for the 2 cents each deposit. He bought and read everything printed in paperback about "Escape, evasion, and impersonation".

Another "Marital Asset" that was awarded to his mother (and hence her new husband) was the "Lifetime Lease to the Marital Residence" of the old Dr.'s Mansion on the Cape. Paco felt a curious sense of justice and felt a renewed faith in things spiritual when the following year, after his new stepfather had spent a small fortune on renovations to convert it into a restaurant, hurricane "Carol" wiped the old place off the face of the Earth.

A couple of weeks before Hurricane "Carol" one incident served to clearly establish the parameters of his relationship with his stepfather. Having been as he put it "forced into servitude" Paco was washing dishes in the restaurant for no pay whatsoever, when his stepfather made a comment about not being happy at the quality of the dish cleaning. His stepfather told him that "the poor job" on some of the pots and pans were "typical" of Paco's fathers "poor standards and sloppiness."

Muttering something about "Family Honor" Paco went to his room and returned with a 3 foot Swedish bayonet. The antique bayonet was the length of a dress sword, and had been bought by Paco, with a few dollars of his "shellfishing" money by mail order through an ad in "Popular Mechanics Magazine". Brandishing the naked blade he threatened to "run his stepfather through," and said that "no one could talk about his father that way and live".

The stepfather was genuinely frightened. After much hubbub with his mother intervening and his brother cheering him on a "Modis Vivendi" was achieved and a resulting agreement stipulated that the stepfather would "Keep his goddamn mouth off of Paco's Dad", and the bayonet (and his knives) would remain sheathed and packed away. His mother pleaded "can't we just live a normal life?' "Sure" said Paco who bought a guitar and drove his stepfather nuts playing all of his dad's old favorites over and over and over.

A couple years later, when he was fourteen Paco had had enough of the "normal" life, at his stepfather's house and had left home. The actual leaving part was precipitated by a prolonged period of Paco's "skipping school". He would leave for school each day but instead of going he would take the Subway downtown and go to the movies or better yet the museums. Students were admitted free and it was safer then the school in his stepfather's neighborhood.

With its race wars, gang fights, and student "protection rackets" the neighborhood High School was a dangerous place. You could get really hurt if you didn't pay up. When Paco "the new kid" refused to pay he was thrown down a flight of stairs and hospitalized with head injuries. He continued to refuse to pay and was thrown into a lake that was near the school. He still wouldn't pay so he was attacked and beaten senseless in the vestibule of his church. When he was assaulted coming out of a store one afternoon he retaliated and for once beat up his attacker. (He was learning). The Neighborhoods were all divided into "gang turf". Switchblades weren't legal but were available and very popular.

In self-defense he became friends with a cop's son who was "unaffiliated and didn't want to be". He and his friend had teamed up and survived by carrying large hunting knives (which trumped switchblades). When others followed suit they had "borrowed" pistols from their parents. Paco took a revolver (a snubnose 32 hammerless Smith and Wesson) from the bottom drawer of his stepfather's bedside table. After finding it one day Paco had wondered whether his stepfather kept in fear of his father or him. In any event the case was dusty and wasn't checked on regularly.

He and his friend, who had "borrowed" his fathers 38 Caliber Colt Police Service Revolver went out walking for a few nights and "trespassed" on all the turf of all the local gangs. Each time they were attacked they flashed the revolvers and the punks melted away.

When he was finally caught by the "truant officer" after a couple months of no show at school his stepfather was exultant. "They have a special school for kids like you with locks on the doors." It was called "disciplinary school" and Paco had heard all about it.

Paco opted to decline the opportunity to attend the aforementioned institution, and after withdrawing his life's savings ($70.00) from "The Boston 5 cent savings bank", he split.

 Hitchhiking around the country he acquired a knack for regional accents, and a real empathy for the poor and downtrodden. The people he hitched with became his friends, roll models, and mentors. Perfect strangers would unburden their hearts to him and he listened to their troubles and could always see their view and counsel them. It was a good experience. They gave him good life advice too, from fixing cars to parenting. Many who had been down and out counseled "you can always go to a restaurant and ask to work for a meal. There's no shame in that". Paco did often and ate fairly well.

Many of them were paternal and concerned. Quite a few told horror stories of the chain gangs in Georgia that were very much still operational at the time, and told him never to hitchhike in the state of Georgia. After hearing many such stories he always stood on the state line and waited for a ride going all way through. Avoiding police attention became habitual. He was counseled that if he was left on the near side of a town he should always walk through and never to hitch within city limits. He always did.

Before he would accept a ride he would look carefully for a moment at the driver and try to judge how much danger he was in. The roads of America and especially the Deep South were crawling with drunks and perverts. Learning to exercise good judgment was a necessary survival skill and he quickly learned when to be cautious. After a while he could just "see inside" people.

It was fortunate that in general the perverts were cowards and when molestation was attempted Paco would display the handle of the knife and tell them to stop the car and let him out. They always did, but he was often alarmed and lived in a wary "heightened state" of consciousness. As a result his senses became acute. He learned to "read" people. As he traveled over a period of time he developed what would later be characterized as "spider senses" It was later said that he could "see around corners".

Many a time he played "Dixie" or "Yellow rose of Texas" on his harmonica to sooth some savage beast. It was a good set of skills, listening, counseling, mimicking, and distracting with music. One of his first stops had been in Nashville where he haunted "the Grand Ol Opry". He had grown up listening to them late into the night on a crystal radio set which he had kept concealed in his mattress since he was 6 years old. Now, not that many years later he would play harmonica with many of the old-time stars at an outdoor festival. He played Arkansas Traveler and Turkey in the Straw with Grandpa Jones.

A few times in the Deep South he was stopped by police but always had a ready explanation for his presence and always claimed to be only 50 miles from his "pappy's" and on his way home. Suspicious of his youth they had been disarmed by a rousing rendition of "Dixie", and had always let him continue.

In Alabama and Louisiana he rode for two days at 20 miles an hour with a creaking carload of redneck oil workers who taught him to roll a cigarette one-handed.

He got picked up late one night on a road in Mississippi in the still segregated south. The old cracker driver was wild on moonshine and nearly killed them driving seventy and eighty, weaving and pulling his model "A" up behind cars with northern plates, flashing his lights, shooting his pistol and cackling.

On one occasion in Miami he had been arrested as a vagrant and spent an unpleasant few days in "the Dade County Youth Hall".

The admitting Officers were not at all pleased to find Paco's razor sharp bone handled 5 inch bladed hunting knife strapped under his shirt and muttered dire threats. (Their favorite threat was quite graphic and involved insertion of acid into the rectum.) He was forced to consume his entire bowl of "grits" without water, (grits, gack) and listened while a child was beaten a few cells down for "unauthorized pissing". (There were no toilets in the cells.)

A "juvenile detective" who was bringing him to court the following Monday to be "fingerprinted, processed, and interviewed", left him unattended at a gas station for a few minutes. The "detective" had not bothered to handcuff him and sitting in the passenger's seat Paco at first had checked out the glove compartment. Seeing a 38 Caliber Revolver lying there 14 year old Paco had a flash of paranoia. Why was this cracker leaving him alone with a gun? Was he really that stupid or was it a trap? Paco looked over and saw the "detective" earnestly talking to someone in the garage and wasn't looking.

Wisely not touching the gun he had eased the door open and slipped away. He hid in a culvert for several hours. Eventually emerging after nightfall he went to the bus station where his suitcase had been checked. Retrieving it he stopped into a pawnshop for a new knife and then caught a ride north.

On another occasion he was picked up in Glendale, California and held for a couple days at the Burbank City Jail. He called his employed older brother who wired money for a bus ticket. While waiting for the wire to arrive the cops had been entertaining "the kid" by showing him their shoulder holster rigs. They didn't buy him an ice cream cone but they did get him boxed meals, and let him watch them book the hookers they dragged in on a Saturday night. When the money for a bus ticket back east came he was given a ride to the bus station with the siren on and the red light flashing. They even let him keep his knife.

Eventually he would return home, but as an emancipated person. He had won his freedom. He lived in their house on his own terms and came and went as he pleased. He renewed contact with his father. Applying for and getting a set of working papers" (that were required for juveniles under 16) he got a job in a warehouse lifting crates and boxes. He paid a nominal rent to his mother, and ate his meals at school and at work. He made enough to date and dance and although busy had a lot of fun while working his way through high school.

Two things happened that made Paco very glad that he had gone through the entire experience

One was that in the entire history of his high school only two students had run away to Florida and only one to Los Angeles. Paco had done both. By "breaking the school record" he so impressed the crusty old "Drill Major", who was in charge of the Compulsory High School ROTC program in existence at the time, that he promoted Paco to "Acting Brigadier General" whereupon "General Paco" led four thousand marching students in Boston's annual "Schoolboy Parade".

 The other thing happened a few weeks after he had come back. He was coming out of a store near Codman Square in

South Boston when he was surrounded and accosted by the most feared, infamous and toughest gang in the entire area. "The Deadly Dozen".

At least nine of the dozen had him pinned into an alcove. "HEY PACO" the leader said. This was some serious shit. "We hear you can roll a cigarette one-handed" it was more of an accusation then a question. "Welllll yah," said Paco. "Show Us" it was an order not a request. So Paco did. Carefully removing a cloth bag of "Bull Durham" from his shirt pocket with the thumb ring finger of his right hand he tugged the bag open with his teeth assisted by his index finger.

Taking a cigarette paper from the same pocket with the index and middle fingers he creased it and with the bag balanced on the back of his hand tipped tobacco into the creased paper. Carefully holding the tobacco loaded creased paper without spilling Paco drew the string on the bag closed with his teeth and replaced the bag in his pocket. With the rest of the fingers of his hand now free he held the paper with his index and ring fingers and packed the tobacco into a tube shape with his middle finger. With his thumb he pushed against the packed tobacco in an upward motion and rolled it up into a cigarette. Licking the edge of the paper he finished the seal. It was pretty scraggly looking but it was definitely a functional cigarette. "The trick is not to spill any", said Paco and fishing a match from his pocket, he lit it.

The "Deadly Dozen" were very impressed, "Wayyyy Cool Paco" the leader said "your alright". He was never bothered again, by any of the gangs.

When he finished High School he decided he wanted to go to college away from Boston and did so.

CAMBRIDGE 1963

Maya met Paco in the fall of 1963 at a coffeehouse in Cambridge.

She had seen Paco the previous spring at a benefit that Paco had staged in Boston. Just to celebrate life (and his first acid trip) Paco had hired the Hatch Memorial Shell and had produced a "Hootenanny" that had gone on for 72 hours. Narrowly skirting a Public assembly prohibition called "The Marathon Law" which prohibited "Marathon performances" of more than three days Paco figured that if more than three days was illegal that three days must be legal. After hiring a platoon of Boston's finest for "Security" The show went on.

Every performer from New York to Maine had showed up. And with the radio stations in full support with 20-minute updates and plenty of TV coverage for the entire 3 days the crowds had been great. They were so great (and a little unruly) that the Police Chief of Boston swore that Paco would never stage another event in his town. It had been a big success however, and raised a barrel of money, which was donated to a Children's Fund at a local hospital.

Maya attended the concert and noticed him making announcements. She was curious, who was this guy, what was he about. He certainly wasn't like any of the other guys she knew. She asked around. She liked what she heard. At the concert Paco had noticed her too.

Up until that time Maya had regarded her future as a foregone conclusion. To her parents great relief (god forbid she should take up with a musician) she had finally agreed to marry a Dr. who was interning at some teaching facility, and who drove a Morgan sports car. Maya tended to sum up men by what they drove. Her previous boy friend had been a skydiver with a raggedy jeep, jeans, and leather jacket to match. She had called him "the Jeep". Her parents had met him and contemplated jumping out the window of their high rise Manhattan apartment. Her father carried a gun and had a permit because he owned an upscale Manhattan clothing business that serviced most of the foreign embassies and often dealt in cash. For years he had been pulling back his coat to display his gun to Maya's dates and with a raised eyebrow would advise them to "have her home on time". Her "parental approved" fiancée drove a Morgan and in an indefinable way looked like a Morgan with his tweed jackets, and pipe. Guess I'm gonna marry a Morgan she thought fatalistically.

Because her fiancée was off on a sabbatical or something this particular fall night in Cambridge a mutual friend escorted her. This was a local D. J. whose professional name was Bob J. Lutchmuck ("making hay with Robert Jay"). He had the hot's for her but had callously left her unattended while he went off to meet, greet, and schmooze. Paco saw her and knowing the DJ to be a major sleazoid as well as being the poster child for "slow talkers of America" he just sat down and said "Hi baby". They had wound up leaving together. He drove her home and she gave him her number. She wanted to know who he was and the more she found out the more she liked him.

She was a stunning graduate Arts Major who had grown up in uptown Manhattan and had lived in Spain as an exchange student. She loved to go to museums. She had a flair for fashion, painting, and poetry. Her favorite colors were orange and brown. Her favorite time of the year was the fall.

Paco called her a couple days later and he said, "wanna go to the zoo? They went to the zoo. They went to dinner. They went to the movies. They went to museums. They climbed all over the USS Constitution in Charlestown Harbor. They went everywhere together for the next week or so. When Dr. Morgan returned she broke her engagement.

They became lovers. When he found out her father was not, repeat not happy.

Nothing in Paco's life experience had prepared him for the shock of having this beautiful vivacious, talented, cheerful person in his life. He was transported. She "looked out" for him and covered his back while he worked. She helped him with his "Cash Projections" he had to submit to the banks that financed his instrument purchases. She decorated his, welll, now their apartment and while knocking out gourmet meals always made sure they had time for sex and to read a book. They spent a lot of time in the bookstores around Harvard Square. They spent a lot of time in bed.

Paco's occupation was importing and lecturing on musical instruments from exotic places. He traveled to Mexico, France, and Spain to purchase the output of various Factories and Luthiers and supplied a lot of the area schools and old music societies. Compared to his peers he was affluent.

Although she had acquiesced when father had approved the engagement to the Morgan driving Dr., Paco had swept her off her feet. His music, his international experience, his respect in the community, his back stage access to the local music scene, the all night jam sessions, the cute foreign cars (two Morris Minors and a classic MG), his fundraising in support of Martin Luther King's SNCC (Student non-violent coordinating committee).

Paco took her to meet his Dad. In 1963 his father was remarried to the widow of a Professor of Music at a Brandies University whom he had met on one of his forays into the used bookstores. The professor's widow administered a fund, which produced baroque music concerts. His pop was happily retired and as a hobby rebuilt antique harpsichords and clavier's which he would buy on his annual trips to Europe with the widow who went there every year to administrate the translations of her husbands books on Bach into various languages. It was a cultural home run. They had dinner with the 92-year-old harpsichordist Wanda Landowska and attended Baroque music concerts. They went to plays, and saw all the folk artists. Hanging out with their friends they attended parties with Sandy Bull, Hamza Al Din, Rambling Jack, Joan Baez, Karen Dalton, Mimi and Richard Farina, Jose Feliciano, Buffy Saint Marie, Fred Neil, Bob Dylan, and all the other artists who came through Boston at the time.

Maya later told friends that after dating for a few weeks the defining moment when she fell for him was on an uphill off ramp from Storrow Drive, in Boston. They were stopped at the light waiting when the engine had stalled. Paco tried to start the car with the key but the battery was low and wouldn't turn the engine over. Leaning back in her seat she looked at Paco and wondered "how is this guy going to handle this situation?" Pausing for just a moment to set the hand brake, put the car in neutral, and raise one finger in the "just a moment sign" Paco opened the door went to the trunk and then to the front of the car. Inserting the crank (that came with all Morris Minors) into a hole below the radiator he engaged the driveshaft and gave a quick twirl. The engine sprang into life. Jumping back in he pulled away as the light changed. Maya laughed all the way home.

The previous year one or more Federal Agencies had tried to keep Paco under surveillance in Boston for suspected smuggling activities. It was true that there was a small inner circle of about a dozen guys who took turns re-supplying the others with an occasional ounce of pot. For the few Jazz Musicians and Buffs, and dozen or so students who preferred it the easiest and most cost effective method was driving to New York City.

For much higher points within the peer group (respect is a currency of the young), the more complicated way to gain status was to do a border crossing and return. Whether it was from Paris with a little hash or Mexico with some good pot or even Morocco with it's Cannabis Indicta (kief). Successful completion of a "run" conveyed great status to the successful runner.

Unable to resist the challenge Paco had, on a few occasions, while on legitimate trips abroad, brought in small amounts of various smokables of wildly varying quality. On one early trip to Mexico City Paco, who at that time spoke very little Spanish, had agreed to allow his karate instructor/bodyguard/friend to come along and to use Paco's completely routine business trip as "cover" to bring back a few Kilos.

It was necessary in the dangerous environment of the Federal District of Mexico a.k.a. Mexico City to have extra security. The instructor (who was the black sheep of the Boston Karate

Academy) was called "Sidekick" so named because of his favorite strike, which was a side head kick from a flat-footed standing position. There also was a pro Mexican security guy (called a business agent) that Paco had employed through the U.S. Embassy and who supplied real security and expert translations.

The reason for all this was the cash payments Paco made to the factories and Luthiers that he dealt with (he didn't trust the Mexican banking system). It was world class fun to fly to Mexico City, hang out in "Sanbornes de la Reforma", or on the "Calle Hamburgoso" where the beautiful people of Mexico socialized. In the late evenings there was "La Malinche".

Named after the woman who had been Fernando Cortez's mistress, and had helped him conquer the country with 325 men, it was the largest brothel in the Western Hemisphere. Employing over a hundred women from all over the world, the atmosphere in the grand old mansion was like a party. Four bars, three mariachi bands, wide sweeping staircases and the hundred girls made it a great social center. For a healthy single young man it was sort of a "home away from home".

On this particular trip, while Paco was off touring factories with his "business agent" the Sidekick scored 8 or 10 kilos for about 17 bucks each. They traveled to the border by train in a private compartment and had spent the 24-hour trip cleaning the pot reasoning that there was no point in risking getting busted for seeds and stems.

They spent a comical afternoon riding up and down the Mexican side of the Rio Grand in a horse drawn cart searching the riverbank for a good crossing point and trying to remember the word for shallow. They were shocked to find out there were fresh water crocodiles with remarkably wide jaws in the river.

They went into a border bar to wait for nightfall.

Sitting at a table off to the side and nursing a beer they watched as a little guy at the bar pulled out a small automatic and waved it in the face of a huge classical Mexican bandito type. The big guy just backed away toward the door waving his hands and pleading for his life saying "he had a wife and little ninos". In apparent abject terror the big guy drew the curtain by the door in front of him as though the curtain would protect him somehow. The little guy kept waiving the little gun in the big mans face threatening and enjoying his moment of power. Then the big guy dropped the curtain.

In his hand was a cocked pearl-handled 45. Paco froze, he wanted to tip the table over and hide behind it movie style. The Sidekick demurred, "the noise might set em off" he whispered. The little guy then began backing up and waving the little peashooter off to one side he pleaded and begged for his life. "I have a wife and little ninos," he said. After watching the little guy crap his pants for a while the big guy finally put his cannon away. The moral of the story was "Caliber does make a difference."

Later in the evening the Sidekick had crossed the old-fashioned way swimming the Rio Grand in the middle of the night. With alarm sirens screaming and border patrol agents rushing toward the crossing point it had been a miracle that they had returned safely.

In Paris on a diferent trip Paco, was unable to connect with a small time hash supplier. Oblivious to the political situation, he had taken a side trip to Algeria arriving on the day of Algerian Independence from France. The Port City was crowded with victorious troops, tanks, sub machine guns, and steaming cathouses. He spent a week. After some interesting physical confrontations while hanging around the docks (thank god for the Karate lessons) Paco had scored about a pound of what later was termed "the worst hash ever" and had risked his liberty to bring it back strapped to his body.

On one other trip Paco had concocted a great cover story involving business with a "forwarding agent" and had strapped a kilo to his body and crossed several times at Laredo on foot. He was challenged but had his cover story and some paperwork handy and was not searched. Declining the temptation to try it for a second day, he disposed of several extra Kilos over a garden wall in the old town on the Mexican side. The upshot of the story was that he brought back a one pound envelope of excellent clean pot for everyone in his immediate circle. He often wondered what the owner of the garden had thought when he went out in the morning and found all that pot..

Invariably the pot (or hash) was consumed within the group. At that time there was no other way to get any pot. There was no supply and distribution net work. Organized crime didn't bother with it and a supply system simply didn't exist. For the few local jazz buffs that liked it an old dealer called "Joe the Arab" would make the long drive to NYC and back. In "The City" If one had a friend, one could buy ten and twenty-dollar payroll envelopes filled with very questionable quality pot. Joe the Arab had been at it so long that he still called pot "gage" or "reefer".

One character made a regular semi-annual cross country trip financed by eager members of the fringe community who would "invest" in a "drug-run" in which they would pay in advance for a promised good deal on some pot based on a super good small sample. He would then pocket the money and disappear to the other coast for 6 months. He was a former carnival worker with a jovial manner and full of stories. In the Carney World he had earned the nickname "the Walkaway Kid".

They called him that because he had gotten work at so many carnivals and then, after his change apron was full he would just "walk away". On the rare occasion that he was confronted by one of the victims he would always have a story of "what went wrong". ("I got it but was busted") ("I got it but was robbed") ("I was about to be busted so had to dump it") ("The dog ate it") Often after offering another great sample he would talk them into a second "investment" with the promised return even better than the first. In a worst case scenario he would display any one of a number of weapons he kept secreted about or near his person at all times and would walk away.

Another Character was "The Mad Scientist". As young man he had become addicted to morphine while serving as a medic in the Army. The Mad Scientist became a specialist in acquiring drugs and extracting drugs from any preparation or compound that contained them. At first he bought them, but they were expensive and hard to come by. He would have cleaned up and moved on to a healthier life but his slattern of an "old lady" wouldn't hear of it. She wanted her dope. It was all she wanted and she had no other source.

More to please her than to feed his own needs the Scientist became a Pete Man. (safecracker) Hiring muscle to help him the diminutive "mad Scientist" would break into factories and warehouses usually on the eve of payday. Taking most of the night to do so and with the aid of hydraulics and pry bars they would literally "crack" the safe and get access to the cash inside. He would spend the cash on drugs. The down side was that when he got caught he would be sentenced to long stretches in prison. The upside for him was that his old lady who was desperate for drugs and had no other sources would seduce and sleep with members of the state legislature who would then lobby for his release.

This worked a couple of times, but as soon as he was out his girl friend would torment him with "get me some dope". The potential length of prison time involved was daunting and so the Mad Scientist changed his Modis Operendi. He decided to "eliminate the middle man" rather than stealing cash and then trying to buy drugs he would just steal drugs. The penalties were a lot less (petit v grand larceny), so accordingly he began to specialize in drug stores.

Entering at night from the floor above through a hole he would cut in the roof (or the floor of a vacant apartment above) he would then lowered down by his hired muscle. He would spend hours inside reading labels and retrieving a large carton of not only the obvious narcotics and Merck coke but also any chemical compound that could be converted or extracted into usable dope. Hence the nick name "the Mad Scientist". Each occasion resulted in a weeklong party.

One evening Paco had stopped by and raptly watched as a tiny ball of pure opium was extracted from some other compound and was consumed in the traditional Chinese manner. Holding the little ball of pure brown Opium on the end of a metal rod in place of the traditional pipe he had turned it spinning while heating it over an alcohol flame. At one point the tiny ball expanded and then became a wisp of smoke suspended in the quiet air of the room blue, tangible, and separate from the surrounding air. The Mad Scientist leaned in with a soda straw, and with a deft sip the suspended smoke disappeared. That's how its done he said with a happy grin. Eventually his old lady left him for another guy that was robbing drugstores at gunpoint at the time and thus could supply more drugs faster. The Mad Scientist had finally had enough. He cleaned up his act and eventually hooked up with a nice lady who helped him stay that way.

There was one character who used no drugs whatsoever and was, in Paco's opinion, the most interesting of all. It was "Professor Jacques". The "Professor" was a multi talented genius renegade Frenchman. He had originally come to MIT as a student but upon somehow gaining access to the computer mainframe he had changed his status (in the computer) to Professor. While he was at it he assigned himself a laboratory, a telephone line, a listing in the Faculty

Directory, and three passes to the Faculty Dining room. One for him and two for his "guests". He also had the computer issue him a salary check with per diem expenses.

When not in his "Laboratory" He lived in one of the St. Botolph Street Lofts that were later torn down to make the entrance ramp to Copley Square. He flew his girl friend "Ella" in from France and they had a great time.

Whenever he was questioned about his specialty by another Faculty Member he would wave his arms and shake his shaggy head as he explained some obscure scientific principle in rapid fire idiomatic French. You would have to understand Boston to believe that no one was so impolite that they would admit that they hadn't a clue what he was talking about. He fit right in.

He often entertained Paco and his Brother at the Faculty Dining Room and was always available as a "reference". Paco would be asked from time to time while traveling to provide a reference. He would always give the number of his good buddy Professor Jacque. Whoever was checking whether it was a US Embassy, a foreign police agency, or just a car rental place would call the MIT switchboard and ask for " Professor Jacque please" The operator would check the Faculty Directory and connect them with the "Professors Laboratory". The "Professor" would then give a glowing reference in regard to his esteemed colleague Mr. Paco. It was a terrific resource.

Paco's brother was no slouch. He too accessed the main frame and using it to calculate odds he opened a bookmaking operation that took bets on the horses and greyhounds from the more affluent students. This was so successful that it led to a visit from a colorful gentleman known as "Big Louie". Big Louie informed Paco's Brother "det him and da boys had been watching his operation and were reeel impressed". They were so impressed that "dey were inviting him into their "Family". Of course he would have to take his turn doing jail time like everyone else. "He din hafta of course he could go out of business, no hard feelings." Paco's brother who already was a "computer whiz" and who had a promising future as a molecular scientist opted to shut down. They were all very impressed with "Big Louie", and took pains never to cross him.

Another character was "The Shadow". A popular joke at the time was "who knows what evil lurks in de heart of de man." Answer: "De Shadow do". It was The Shadow's activities that were about to affect the lives of Paco and Maya. The brilliant son of a professor, the Shadow had grown up in the University environment. Living for a while in the communal house that Dr Timothy Leary had maintained near Boston at the time the Shadow was the first of their peer group to get his hands on pure Sandoz LSD. That and an incredible discovery of an entire field of wild marihuana had catapulted the Shadow into the front rank of the drug culture at the time. Since the wild pot wasn't very strong the Shadow (who was a member of the small "pot circle") elected to try his hand at a Mexican border crossing.

He was caught in Laredo Texas with a Kilo of clean pot strapped to his body. In those days it was an automatic 5-year penalty. They were friends, so Paco went his bail, putting up his business as security.

After the Shadow fled the country to avoid the 5 years in jail the scrutiny became intense. Paco and Maya were followed everywhere, Maya's parents joined in the hue and cry and came to Boston to make credible dire threats against Paco (who was now living with Maya).

Maya's father hat put together a "dossier" on Paco, and was funding detectives to dig up whatever they could. The Fed's buzzed like angry bees. Several lawyer friends, who had Federal Practices, including the famous F. Law Bigwig (whom Paco had hired for The Shadow) told him he was in deep do-do. Even with switching cars and ducking the wrong way down one way streets it was becoming difficult to just hang out.

One day while on a trip to NYC to arrange for a sale to a jobber of several dozen dulcimers he had manufactured in Mexico and imported Paco heard on a passing car radio about the shooting in Dallas. Taking the shuttle back to Boston the flags were all at half-mast when the plane arrived. It was the end of an era. The country was in shock and no one wanted to buy exotic instruments. The creditors and heat were tightening their grip.

It was time to go.

SPAIN

After the JFK murder, Paco closed his business. He sold one of the Morris Minors and the MG, and put the other Morris in storage. Taking what cash they had, over her parents "vigorous objections", they had left the country together.

Well, vigorous wasn't quite the right word for it; Maya's father accompanied by a Corporate CEO friend who also had a gun came up to Boston and held Paco at bay while they packed their daughter into a limo and took her back to NY.

Where there is love there is a way. By having her ex college roommate call the parents house Paco re-established communications with the incommunicado "kidnap victim' who, it turned out, was being held in her uncles house in Tenafly, New Jersey.

A couple nights later Maya climbed (with two suitcases of clothes and a makeup case) out the rear bedroom window of her uncle's house and into a waiting taxi whereupon she met Paco at JFK Airport. Paco had also packed two suitcases for her from the things she had left at his apartment, plus one for himself and his guitar made 7 pieces of luggage.

They took the night prop plane to Iceland. It was the cheapest flight available at the time and connected through to Brussels after a four-hour stop in Goose Bay, Canada, and a morning bus trip into the center of Reyavalic, Iceland for an elaborate breakfast while the plane was being refueled. The entire flight took nearly 24 hours but Icelandic Airlines fed them well and constantly so they napped and ate looking down at the polar ice cap below. They were warm and content.

Finally arriving from Brussels in Paris they got a hotel on the left bank and discovered the custom of "hot chocolate in bed in the morning" It had a tendency to make them stay in bed most of the day. It was like a honeymoon.

After a few days they made their way through France by train to Barcelona, Spain. Making love in their private compartment was enhanced by the random lurch of the speeding, rocking train. For a week Paco toured instrument factories. Maya with her language skills found that she could be employed teaching English.

Working there way south they stayed several weeks in Valencia

In Valencia Maya was the cause of several auto accidents as passing drivers were so distracted by her figure that they drove into things, other cars, and off the road. She had to stop wearing the knit suits that were popular at the time. The visiting sailors of a US aircraft carrier voted her Ms. Kittyhawk or whatever the name of their ship was. It was all interesting and fun.

Their happiness was reflected in Paco's Music. A passionate aficionado of Flamenco, Paco studied with a teacher in Valencia who ran a meat market in the daytime and taught "Old Style" Flamenco at night. As a result Paco could play a very credible Alegrias, a little Soleares, some Segudillas,

Tarrantas, and the Farruca. His prize possession was a lovely old Ramirez Guitar. It delivered hauntingly beautiful music with the lightest touch.

Working there way south from Barcelona, they stayed a month in Valencia and then continued south into Andalucia.

Passing through Murcia they arrived in Granada and for a few days rented a pension near the "Plaza Nueva". They explored the Albaizin and Sacramonte neighborhoods and were fascinated by the diverse amount of flamenco emanating from the caves in the hills above the city.

They liked it so much they rented a house for 65 dollars a month high up in the in the Albaizin (the old Arab neighborhood) that overlooked the immense "Alhambra fortress". They adopted the local life style. In the days they would arise early and walk through the narrow cobblestone streets to the market. In the afternoon they would "Siesta". (It was a great opportunity to make love) In the evening on their balcony they would watch the twinkling lights of the city down below and listen to the guitars and songs drifting up from the caves.

In the caves of the "Bario Sacramonte" they danced and played all night with the Calo Gypsies who sang "Bulerias" "Fandangos" "Tangos", "Tarantos" and "Granadinas".

Maya learned a few words of their Sanskrit based language. She translated as an old woman would tell the oral tradition stories about how they, The Calo Gypsies, were not the same as the "Romany's" from Eastern Europe that arrived in southern France in the 17th century. The Calo gypsies, she explained, had been in Spain for more than 1200 years. The old Woman (her name was Maya too) told how the present day gypsy family's had originally been kidnapped as prizes of war and brought to Granada by the moors from the provinces of Bengal and Madras in India. They were highly valued as talented musicians, dancers, and artisans, as well as immensely proud and brave. She explained that that was why nearly all the great bullfighters were from prominent Calo Gypsy families.

Many brave Calo men had been recruited in the 15th and 16th centurys to fight the Flemish wars and had been given special papers which exempted them and their families from the expulsions, slavery and oppression of the time. Hence the origination of the phrase "los Flamencos". In the 17th Century, when Washington Irving stepped out onto his balcony at the Alhambra Fortress, and inquired what the music was that came from the "Barrio Sacramonte" on the opposite hill he was told "Es los Flamencos". Thus a word for the music was born in his writings. Flamenco. It stuck.

Bringing her index finger forward from her right eye she made a little circle with the finger which meant look all directions. Then laying her finger beside her nose in the sign that meant "confidential" the old woman beckoned Maya closer. She whispered "Mary Magdalene was a Calo Gypsy". She carried the "Santa Sangre" (the holy Blood) when she arrived during the month of May at Santé Marie de la Mar in southern France early in the mid first century and that she had been accompanied by Lazarus, Jesus mother Mary, and the maimed but risen Christ. The old woman said that Christ had lived among the Calo's and had many children which explained, she said, why they were so talented, bright, beautiful and brave.

One night Paco and Maya went to a cave deep underneath a house in the heart of the "Albaizin". The cave of "Pepe de La Mancha" was the home of a circle of Dancers singers, Guitarist's, and "Palmadores" (handclappers) that had been gathering at the same spot for several centuries. The doors would open at 12:30 AM on Sunday morning and the singing and dancing and sharing of food and drink in "Celebration of the Sabbath" would continue past dawn. Only Gypsies were allowed.

On this evening Paco and Maya came in a little early (12:15 AM) and sat on old chairs near the bar. Paco said "hola" and Maya chattered for a minute with "Pepe" in her musical Castilian. More Gypsies arrived and some began to mutter and stare at Paco. Finally one came over. Drawing a long knife from his sleeve the man said, "many people come here to try and get next to our sweet innocent woman." "When they do," the man said "we do a little cut and chop". As he said this, a second long knife appeared out of the other sleeve. "Then we do a little Flamenco Dance on their corpses out on the street."

"Gulp" said Paco.

Pepe intervened from behind the bar. "Its ok" he said. This guy (referring to Paco) is a student, wait he'll play something for you. Paco said "si comono pero no tengo guitar" (sure but I don't have a guitar.) Its alright said Pepe we have the "house guitar". Paco was very nervous, he knew about the "house guitar" kept in most Spanish Flamenco bars. It was usually used as a drum to keep the "compas". The strings would be dead and a half inch off of the fretboard. He was handed the house instrument. and thought for a moment "maybe it won't be so bad". He saw the hungry look on a young kids face across from him who was eagerly looking forward to watching the "payo" getting cut up and thrown out. Looking up at the circle of hostile faces Paco tried a chord. It was worse. There were no wrappings on the strings. None, just the inner threads. It made no sound.

Lifting his finger he asked Pepe "ay un capo?" (Do you have a capo?) "Si" said Pepe and handed an old fashioned peg driven capo over the bar. Paco attached the capo to the second fret twirling the fretboard shortening device into place and tightening the peg with a deft twist. He tried a chord again. Still no sound, still no wrappings. Sweat broke out on his forehead. Attaching the capo to the fourth fret, further up the neck, Paco tried again.

Like a fine tuned race-car the instrument sprang to life. The action was low and fast, the strings had wrappings. Paco realized that this instrument had been playing traditional flamenco for many years. He played through the first compass of Soleares and slowly let the rhythm build in the traditional way. "Guappa" (sexy) said a woman at the bar. He ran up the bass line and did a series of arpeggios landing back on the 10th beat of the 12 beat compass in perfect time. "Ole" said the man standing over him as he put his knives down on the bar. "Valle" (valid) yelled a woman at the bar.

Paco started a series of tremolos descending through the phyrigian chord changes always coming back to the rhythmical marker which defined the "Palo". He noticed the kid's mouth was open and he was staring. He sensed a buzz and knew the old guitar was singing sweetly for him. He closed out the piece and looked up. "Bravo" said Pepe. All the others agreed. "What else can you play?" said Pepe. One after another Paco played Alegrias, Seguidilles, The Farruca and Tarantos. (Everything he had learned in Valencia) Then he thrust the guitar out into the center of the circle holding it by it upright by the neck in the traditional way. It is time for some one else to play now he said.

"El es une Jaleador" said Pepe, and there was a murmur of assent. A Jaleador was the person who played first in an evening and would call the spirits (duendes) to the cave or fire to listen and assist with creating the magic circle. It was into this circle created by the pulse of the clapping hands, guitars and the passionate singing of the old songs that the woman and men would jump into. Overcome by the energy created in the center they would draw the spirits into themselves and then explode in dance. It was awesome to be in the presence of.

It was a great moment. It was the best moment of his musical life.

Later in the evening the woman from the bar who had seen him play came over and with Maya translating said to Paco. "We have been here every Sunday morning for more than 800 years. We see in your shining eyes the truth of your love for our music. We want you to know that you will always be welcome here. You can always return and fill the cup of your soul from our flowing water (of music)".

Maya pointed out hours later that no one had touched his tuning or capo position. They sang and played and danced and clapped till dawn.

Later in life Paco would see Pepe again. He was warmed to the bottom of his soul when the old man remembered him and asked to hear the five pieces Paco had played that night in the cave. The old man asked for them one by one by name in the original order proclaiming to a cave packed with Gypsies that "this is how to play the old way"

After the experience at Pepe's Paco and Maya were part of the neighborhood. They didn't realize it at the time but they were becoming what the Gypsies called "Gitanandod" (acculturated to the Gypsy way of life.)

On one of their last evenings above Granada Paco was by himself and was descending the crooked narrow cobblestone steps on his way to the "Cueva Bulerias" (Cave of the Bulerias). He had been to several great evenings there and was hoping that this evening would be another.

As he descended he had to pass through a group of young gypsy men. They reminded Paco vaguely of "the Deadly Dozen" of his youth. It was true they this group was the equivalent gang for the barrio. As Paco passed he said "Buenos" and several said "Buenos" in return;

As he continued his descent he could hear their voices behind him. "Quien es el" (who is he) "Oh el", (oh him) "El es el Jaleador" (It's the spirit caller.)

Moving on to Seville they stayed at a "pension" in the "Barrio Triana" in Seville. Paco played with a Gypsy Café Band that played for other gypsy's. The venue was always packed. The rhythm and the dancing of the Sevillanas alternated with the "cante hondo" (deep song) singing of "Solea de Triana" and would go on till four in the morning always concluding with a solemn hymn to the virgin of the Quadalquivir River. They ate Paella, read books to each other, drank thick hot chocolate in bed, smoked a little pot and made love pretty much constantly.

One night the "Queen of the Triana" put her hand on Paco's shoulder, which meant; "these words are for you" and sang a long "Solea". In the words of the song she described the "long lost Gypsy Prince" who was lost to them hundreds of years before. "The blood calls" she said and "it was the blood that had drawn Paco and Maya to their culture."

TANGIER

Running very low on money the young couple had heard of an expatriate colony living on the cheap in the Arab quarter of Tangiers in Morocco. Since they were already familiar with the Arab culture from living in the "Albaizin" they decided to go. Paco was curious about the music and Maya was just plain curious. They had taken a 3rd class train to Algeciras, and after a boat ride, arrived in North Africa with seven pieces of luggage and $7.00 dollars (that's seven).

Only the young, in love and confident set out on international adventures with so little money hoping that life will provide. Opportunities to survive present themselves on a fairly regular basis and could be factored in. Teaching English in Spain, Tour Guide in Morocco. Between them they had many skills. Paco spoke French and Maya was Fluent in Spanish.

Maya suggested they lighten their load. After spreading a
blanket out at the out door "Berber Market" they sold off
three suitcases full of some of their access clothing thus
reducing their luggage load to a suitcase each plus Mayas
paintbox, and Paco's guitar,

This netted them enough for they're first few weeks. It also
resulted in Berber Woman headed out into the Moroccan
deserts and mountains with the latest NY fashions wrapped
around their heads and hanging from their camel saddles and
burros.

The most significant aspect of living in the "casbah" was the
music that poured out from every stall and shop in the narrow
twisted streets. With the rugs hanging out side and the
glittering brass in the shops it gave a thumping punch to the
air. It almost seemed alive with energy. The intense
rhythmical wailing music would saturate the senses and then
overwhelm then again mixing with the pervasive odor of kief
smoke. Then, it would suddenly stop. The call to prayers
would come from the many minarets and the faithful would

obey. It was amazing. The entire culture functioned as one person.

They had survived the rest of the cold rainy winter in Tangier by making small pieces of Hashish out of the local kief for sale for five and ten dollars to the occasional British and American tourists who came off the tour boats looking for pot. This was not particularly easy.

The locals made very poor hash, so it was up to the American and British expatriates to rise to the occasion, form a craftsman's guild, and to turn out some really good quality product. Eager to acquire new skills, and desperately in need of cash Paco and Maya apprenticed themselves to the Hashmakers Guild.

It was a 3-day process to convert two kilos of fresh kief into maybe 60 grams of good hashish.

The first phase involved using a sealed room with butcher paper covering the walls, ceiling and floor. With window screening stretched across a bed frame the truly hard labor of breaking the plant down and separating the tough fibers and stems from the seeds and leaves took a day or so. After removing all the seeds and stems there was a long process of progressively finer screens and then a secret final step which rendered a small pile of pure yellowish resin. The resin turned black as it was compressed into pieces, and the best they could do was a yield of about 30 grams per Kilo.

 The room itself was full of floating resin particles and they often inhaled as much as they scraped from the butcher paper and extraction cloths. Once a week an Arab delivered two kilo bundles of fresh dried kief (that was brought into the city from the hills on donkeys) to a separate house they had maintained in the Casbah and had used to make their Hashish pieces. They would open the door and the bundles would swing out from under the deliveryman's Jellaba as if by magic. The price was two and a half Durham's a Kilo (US $0.50 cents)

Among the pre-hippie expatriate community there were stories of legendary master hashmakers who could extract up to 50 grams per kilo, but their was only one individual who was known to be able to do this at that time and he was tight with his trade secrets. Known in the Arab quarter as a "genius with a hot knife" he worked over an alcohol flame to press the extracted resin into useful shapes. He had been making pieces for a year or so and had a large stash he was planning to bring or have shipped back to NY. That was the easy part, the local police chief would make all the arrangements through the port captain and a ship captain for a small fee.

For Tangier it was just business as usual. The "resident master hashmaker" did help teach Paco and Maya enough so that they were able to survive on the sale of the 50 grams or so they made in a week. On one occasion Paco had made a set of buttons (out of Hash) and had sewn them to his coat. Then, while traveling through France and Spain by train he had slowly carved them up and smoked them. May too contributed to the legends of the Art. The final step in the extraction process involved a rare and particular kind of cloth, which had a unique weave which captured most of the last impurities of leaf fragment from the resin. Maya brought a modern innovation to the process. One day while watching the slow shaking process that was traditional she had a brilliant idea. "Why not use my electric toothbrush?" she said.

They tried it. Making small wire cage with a crank handle, they hooked the electric tooth brush to the other end of the cage and turned it on. The yellow resin flowed onto the piece of butcher paper in a steady even flow, the small vibration was the perfect answer and sped up that step of the process considerably.

One of their peers had taken it much further and had gone off to live in the Atlas Mountains, learned the local Arab dialect's and ultimately became a master grower and hash maker. What an eclectic peer group in the little ex-pat community. Visionaries, poets, criminals, musicians, characters, and pioneers of the drug culture.

Most days a cruise ship would dock in the harbor and after an hour or two inevitably an English, American or German tourist would appear in the "Socco Chico (little square) of the "casbah" (Arab quarter). Usually the tourist would be acting pretty furtive but for a native English speaker it was easy to strike up a conversation.

Upon inquiring where they were from Paco would adopt a confidential tone and warn them that "it was none of his business but if they were looking for pot they should absolutely not score from an Arab." He would go on to explain (absolutely untrue) the tortures and horrors that were inflicted on foreigners for buying pot.

The tourists were completely overwhelmed by the bizarre environment and their own paranoia and upon hearing that the local authorities had a penchant for hanging foreigners upside down, inserting a hose in their rectum and then turning on the water would blanch and stammer. Is was at this point that Paco would reassure them that it was all right they could trust him, after all he was an American not a local and therefore could not be a cop or informant.

By great good fortune Paco would happen to have a small piece of good hash available. In a further effort to augment his clients need for a diversified stash. (After all it was the fabled and exotic port of Tangier) Paco would offer to purchase a small amount of pot from a "trusted source" and taking the ten or 15 dollars/pounds/whatever he would go to the nearest corner grocery stand. There, (out of sight of the tourist) he would buy a one Durham (20 cents US) packet of Kief-Kief (a croissant-sized twist of paper containing about a half ounce of freshly cleaned and finely chopped excellent local pot.) The tourist, who was always entirely unfamiliar with the local price scale, or the fact that pot was essentially legal, went off happy and Paco and Maya would survive for another week.

On the nice days Paco would wake up in their one room "penthouse" and walk to the edge of the roof. Looking down into the harbor he would count the number of cruise ships.

None meant he would go back inside and go back to bed. One meant it was time to get up, have breakfast, and get going. Two or three meant it was time to hurry down to his "office" (an outdoor table) in the café downstairs.

Living deep in the bowels of an Arab Casbah they valued the shared adventure and experience as worth more than the discomfort and poverty.

It wasn't as bad as you might think. There was a black market in Dollars vs. Durham's. Residents of the Jewish community people eager to flee the hardcore Arabic Culture would exchange soft currency Moroccan Durham's for hard currency dollars at a 20% premium. Many of the local people were charming and friendly, some cruel. The music was great and the living was cheap beyond belief. They paid 15 dollars a month for a rooftop room above the "Socco Chico" with running water (outside) and a stunning view of the Port of Tangier. Primitive toilets, dysentery, bedbugs, straw mattresses, and lice were the major drawbacks. They managed to avoid the bedbugs and lice, (Paco got dysentery) and stayed through Ramadan.

The traditional one bowl of greasy vegetable soup a day (for ten cents) was too spicy for their palates, and caused diarrhea from the grease to their sensitive systems, although they gamely drank it on wooden benches in small café's near the "Socco Chico". (Small Square) in the heart of the ancient casbah. After they had been there awhile they found a small Spanish restaurant in the two small rooms of the first floor of an 8th century house in the Arab quarter. There each day they paid 20 cents (US) for a 4-course meal, with an extra ten cents for a half water glass of wine.

 Everybody in both the Arab and expatriate communities smoked all day everyday in long pipes with supsi's (small clay bowls). One of Paco's favorite possessions was a rare stone pipe bowl from Marrakech. At the end of Ramadan things were getting a little dicey, money was still a big problem. They still had a pretty good wardrobe so they would dress for dinner.

Paco had twice made out a blank XYZ Corp. business check with himself as payee for several hundred dollars and signed it G. Peterson Hiccup. He had displayed the checks downstairs at the café and as casually as possible announced "just got these checks from the US in the mail yesterday, yup, looks like our poverty days are over, soon as they clear through the bank. Shouldn't take more than two or three weeks" He would pass them around to be admired by the cadre of admiring street hustlers who worked the same café. Word spread quickly through the Arab Quarter, and based on his new affluent rep he was able to borrow money from two wealthy "trust fund puppies" that were passing through. They gave him their address to send the money to "when his checks cleared."

Shortly after that Paco was sipping mint tea at Abdul Kata's Café across from the Barbara Hutton's house up on the twisted streets hillside streets below the ancient fort. Two things happened.

The first was that he saw the famous old actress herself being helped through her door on two canes. Moments later a miracle happened. Looking over the balcony of the hillside café he saw someone slowly trudging up the steep twisting narrow passage. Fresh off the boat was a Guy Paco knew well from Boston and who, miracle of miracles, owed him a couple hundred dollars. Within a few minutes had collected one hundred of the two, sold a twist of Kief and 3 of his best pieces of hash.

Maya's father's detective arrived at the end of Ramadan. Paco had to admit the guy was pretty good. Apparently Burned Detective Agency hired the best. The mole like individual, who "arrived on the scene" and went under the name Gruff, fastened himself to them.

Paco and Maya had been living under the persona of "The Finchleys" and had been practicing various English accent dialects, mimicking some of the residents and tourists, but it didn't fool Gruff. The detective pulled Paco aside and, disclosing his identity, said "the jigs up are you going to let go of her or are you going to die here?"

They knew that life was fairly cheap in the port city. Just a few weeks before two Germans had killed a guard and escaped from the prison in the old fort at the top of the hill. Unable to find their way through the twisted streets of the casbah down to the harbor and boats they had been recaptured and horribly tortured. Also, stories of knife confrontations were commonplace.

Unlike other North African Countries like Libya, Egypt, and Algeria, Moroccan citizens were all allowed to carry the traditional razor sharp curved dagger worn in the front of their belts. When they heard from Gruff that Maya's father was enroute with a bag of money and a gun Paco and Maya huddled and weren't sure what to do. One thing was for sure, where the Burned Detective Agent was, Maya's father would be, and the Feds wouldn't be far behind. Bowing to the inevitable they decided their best shot was to split up and meet back in the states.

One small chore was to divide their remaining stash of hash. Giving Maya several of their best "fingers" Paco had taken a couple small odd shaped pieces. He put together about half a pound of their lesser grade flat pieces into the false bottom of the pick compartment of his guitar case. He pocketed one little finger sized stick of hash that he had been carving on to smoke, and sewed the set of two hash buttons onto his coat.

Having heard that the Shadow was playing Bass at a Jazz Club in London Paco decided to head north before returning to the States.

Waiting until a few hours before Mayas father's plane arrived he slipped out of the country overland through the tiny North African Port of Ceuta, which was the last toehold of Spain on the African Mediterranean Coast located 30 or 40 miles east towards Libya. From there he caught a boat to Algeciris where he could make a call to the states.

His brother wired him a few hundred dollars and he started north.

Maya skillfully manipulated her horrified father (he was totally disoriented by the environment) into a new wardrobe of the finest Arab materials. With Maya fresh from the hairdressers in the European quarter and wearing a Jellaba fit for a princess and soft pointed shoes they had returned on a first class flight and swept through customs.

Prior to leaving Tangier Maya had removed the talcum from a large can in her fathers shaving kit and had replaced it with her collection of high quality "fingers" of hash. After their arrival in New York she retrieved it.

She was now a full-fledged member of the drug cultures inner circle. She was also a member in good standing of the "International Hashmakers Guild". She had arrived. She was what was "cool, and hip". When she slipped away from her parents and returned to Cambridge she was welcomed as a member of the inner circles and had an aura of beauty and mystery (as well as some of the best hash anybody had ever seen or heard about). She was emancipated. She was hot.

Paco, on the other hand, was up to his ass in alligators. It turned out that the detective Gruff had become aware of where he was going and what he was carrying and had made sure Interpol, and The British Customs Service were alert, notified, and waiting for him.

LONDON

The Landlady stole his hash. Paco couldn't believe it. He had been out to see if the wire had arrived from his brother and when he came back to the little pension he had rented for a dollar a day in Algeciris it was missing. It wasn't his whole stash, just the hash stick he had been smoking off. The rest was concealed in a false bottom of the pick compartment of his guitar case. There was also the two "hash buttons" that were sewed to his coat and looked like real buttons. (They had been lacquered to heighten the illusion) He was sure he had left the stick in his spare pants pocket folded on a chair in his room. He confronted the concierge. "You went through my room" he said, "you took something of mine". She wasn't intimidated, or apologetic, she intended to keep what she had taken and if he had a problem with it she could call Spanish Customs and maybe they could help him sort it out. Paco let it go. It was only one piece, but his troubles were just beginning.

One tip-off he got was when he entered Gibraltar, or rather tried to in order to get his money from the English bank his brother had wired the money to. He had gone over everyday on the little ferry, and each time had been refused admission. Each time they had refused him entry on the grounds that he didn't have enough money for an onward journey. Before they sent him back each day they would spend several minutes examining his passport under infrared lights, examining the staples that held it together and bending it in various directions while holding it up to sunlight. "Just routine" they said.

Eventually a wire arrived in Algeciris to inform him that he had money waiting in Gibraltar and he was finally admitted onto "the rock". He booked a flight for London and boarded. The flight went to Madrid where he changed planes for London.

Arriving at Heathrow, he had been climbing a long outdoor ramp crowded with the people from his flight elbowing their way up toward a gate at the top, which led to a long corridor and "Baggage Inspection". Off to his left there was a similar ramp, which was also crowded with passengers leaving for another flight. Moving down the ramp to the left moving with the human tide were two uniformed British Custom Officials a man and a woman.

"THERES THE ONE WERE LOOKING FOR", yelled the woman, trying to be heard above the general hubbub. "WHERE?" said the man. "OVER THERE" the woman yelled. With her arm extended she was pointing directly at Paco.

At that moment Paco was about 80% of the way up the ramp. It was obvious to him that she had spotted him by his guitar case and glasses. Seeing that what were now his pursuers were caught trying to climb up through the press of the descending crowd on the ramp he put his elbows into high gear and looking to his right slipped his "grandpa" glasses off his face. It changed his appearance. At the top of his ramp another uniformed British Custom Official was oblivious to the frantic activity on the other ramp. His attention was intently focused on each face as it emerged from the ramp into the cool darkness of the crowded passageway. Tangier? He asked, "anyone from Tangier?" The flight had been from Madrid so Paco was sure, in that moment that he, like The Shadow before him, was about to be caught and go to jail. But not quite yet, he was still free for that moment.

Deftly twisting the guitar case out of sight behind his back Paco replied in his best imitation of an upper class British accent "no no my good fellow, Gibrawltor. It worked. The tonality of the accent rang true. Paco, assuming the air of a busy Brit, had simply continued on while the intent Official was trying to cover all the faces emerging from the ramp.

He had bought himself a few seconds more freedom but he could sense in his peripheral vision frantic activity behind him as he walked down the corridor. He slipped a beret from his coat pocket and put it on adopting a long face and stared down his nose at everything in an imitation of Professor Jacque.

It was the staring down his nose that saved him. Instead of going through the door marked with an overhead sign reading "Foreign Nationals" he had blundered to the end of the corridor. Looking for a way to escape Paco opened a door at the end and walked through. Paco could not see very well without his glasses so he had a bewildered look when the official at a desk got up and told him he was in the wrong place. Concerned by Paco's wild-eyed agitation he said, "are you OK"?

Then a miracle occurred "here I have the right stamp for your passport", and reaching into the desk he stamped Paco's passport with a 30 day visa. He was obviously oblivious to the voices and activity going on out in the corridor. The official then opened a side door in his office and Paco exited directly into the very crowded "baggage inspection area".

It was a magic moment. Paco had bypassed passport control. But he wasn't out of there yet, not by a long shot. Paco knew that with his glasses off the other obvious thing they were looking for was someone carrying a guitar. And he still had to get through "baggage inspection". A moment later a porter accosted him and said, "carry your bags guv?" "Mais Certainmant" said Paco. With intense relief he handed over his luggage and moved away from the porter. As they proceeded toward the Inspection Area Paco took advantage of the momentary respite to calm his breathing and tried to slow his heart rate.

Paco figured correctly that these people who had never actually seen him were looking for a tall American with glasses and a guitar case, not a tall Frenchman. The problem now was the guitar case. The porter was confused by the fact that Paco was hanging back as far as possible as though the case contained the plague and was doing everything he could do to distance himself in the crowded reception hall from the incriminating (and half pound containing) guitar case. Thumping the bags onto an inspection bench the porter went off a little confused by this strange Frenchman but satisfied with the ten shillings Paco pressed into his hand. "Merci" Paco said.

The Inspector (one of many) was busy. He glanced at Paco and opened the suitcase and made a couple of cursory pats. Closing it he moved on to the Guitar case. Projecting calmness and boredom Paco raised his eyes toward the ceiling as the inspector opened it and lifting the instrument opened the pick compartment. Paco wondered for a moment it the inspectors had been told to look there in general or whether it was just this guy "reading him". Paco stared of into infinity (his best bored look) when the inspector reached down and, probing, stirred his finger among the capo's, strings, and picks.

He didn't detect the false bottom. A half-pound of Hashish took up a space about an inch thick in a rectangle 4 by 7 inches. He must have assumed the space was filled with padding. He didn't even glance at Paco's coat buttons as he closed the case and made a chalk mark on it and the suitcase. Paco took his luggage and started for the glass doors leading to the street.

Paco was getting panicky again. He was through controls but he was still in the airport, and he was holding the incriminating guitar case. His pursuit couldn't be far behind.

The second miracle of the day happened then. Walking up to the where buses left to into the various destinations in London were dispatched from Paco asked a dispatcher who was standing by a bus, "Is there anywhere I can put my guitar case? Its very fragile" "Righto" the dispatcher said and opened a little side compartment on the bus. Paco put the guitar case into it. Then, saying something about "teatime" the dispatcher left the area.

Boarding the bus Paco had a ray of hope. The guitar case had been the key identifier and without it visible he just might have a chance. He adjusted the angle of his beret, calmed has breathing, and stared down his nose at the floor in his best imitation of a bored Frenchman he waited. One by one some of the buses started to leave.

Out of his peripheral vision he saw a sudden commotion by the glass doors he had come out of. Men in trenchcoats came rushing out. Boarding each bus they rapidly scanned all the faces. Paco stared down his nose at the floor and held his breath. They had a lot of busses to cover (more were revving their engines and were starting to leave) so the CID (Criminal Investigation Division of Scotland Yard) guys in their trenchcoats had a lot of ground to cover in very little time. Of the two that bustled aboard Paco's half-filled bus one franticly scanned the luggage racks while the other looked at faces. Pausing at Paco's seat the second trenchcoat said "American"? Exuding indifference Paco said " Je suis desolate, m'seu. Je ne parle pas anglais" (I'm sorry, I don't speak English) lifting his hands palms up and giving a gallic shrug. (He was still mimicking "Professor Jacque") Paco was apologetic. They were in a hurry. Shifting their attention the men got off the bus and ran to the next one peering everywhere as they went.

Paco's bus pulled out. As he rode into the city Paco could not believe he had gotten away. In a state of semi-shock he stared out the window until the bus pulled up near Victoria Station. He had kept looking back expecting at any moment to see blue flashing lights to come up from behind. None did. When the dispatcher on the Victoria end of the bus run opened the little door on the side of the bus so Paco could retrieve his "fragile luggage" Paco grabbed the guitar case and melted into the crowds of Victoria Station.

Still quite agitated Paco tried to assess his situation as he hurried along really acting quite furtive. Hustling out a side door he walked along a London Street near the Station. It was obvious that they were looking for him. It was equally obvious that they had been told to expect him. It was also obvious that if they didn't catch him in possession of anything they couldn't prove a thing. His first priority was to get in some where and then separate himself from the hash.

He saw a small hotel and rang the bell. There was a small sign on the door "British nationals only". Pretending to be a Brit from out of town, Paco registered. Because he was unfamiliar with England he didn't know what to put down for an address. The concierge was distracted for a moment so Paco made up the name G. Worthington Hickok and flipping back a couple pages back in the registry book he copied an address from a previous page.

Upstairs in his room Paco looked out the heavy drapes at the dreary little side street. He reasoned that if they were looking for an American or Frenchman it would take them a while (if at all) to find him in an English Hotel under an English identity. He concluded that he was safe for the moment.

The adrenaline was still pumping so he did rhythmic breathing, relaxed a little, and began to consider where he could hide his stash. Hiding it in the room was out of the question. If it was in his room "ipso facto" it was his. He decided to hide it elsewhere in the Hotel. If it was found it could be anybody's. After all it was a transient hotel.

Waiting until he heard no sound in the hallway Paco crept out and reconnoitered. He finally decided that the least likely place to be disturbed was behind the facings of the new carpeting on a little used flight of stairs leading to the roof. So over the next hour Paco stashed the flat pieces, and a few odd "finger pieces" behind the carpet. Back in his room Paco felt truly safe.

Carving a tiny corner off one of his buttons he had a pipe and his spirits lifted. It was because he felt so safe that Paco put on a British looking tweed jacket and decided to go out and see the town.

He made a list of jazz clubs from the phone book and a couple of jazz publications that were at a newsstand. Figuring that it wouldn't be long before he ran into his friend if he just "hung out on the scene" He first went to the largest and best-known Club. He was sitting quietly having a cup of coffee when the door literally burst open. "The Flying Squad" of Scotland Yard entered the place like gangbusters. "Everybody stay where you are!" "Jeeeese" thought Paco "these guys are really pissed". He briefly wondered whether it was a coincidence or, if not, how they had found him so fast.

Going from person to person they searched everyone in the place. They were really thorough. The detective who searched Paco from head to toe looked in the seams of his clothing and his hat. He probed every pocket but found nothing. Paco's papers were in order (he had the visa) and he wasn't in possession of any contraband. Welll there was the buttons but his coat was back at the hotel. So they left.

Paco was really shaken. It was like a nightmare that wouldn't end. He returned to the hotel and barely left for a week. The hotel brought meals on a tray at breakfast and teatime, so it was a good chance to rest and recover from the Tangier winter.

After a few days he ventured forth again and explored the city. His furtive manner attracted attention and he was constantly entering stores by one door and leaving by another and changing buses to throw of any possible surveillance. The flying squad had really unnerved him. One day he took different random trains all day to "wear out" any possible tail.

(After all he wasn't Jack the Ripper). Eventually he felt more comfortable.

After a week of haunting the Jazz scene he ran into someone he knew and who knew The Shadow. "He's in Tangier".

Paco left the stash in the hotel behind to be retrieved on some other journey and headed south first by ship from Dover to Calais then by rail through France and Spain back to Algeciris. When he crossed the final border headed south he had smoked almost all of both buttons. He put the last fragment inside an orange and ate it as he passed through customs back to Tangier.

He found his friend living in a villa in the European section. It was a brief reunion. In order to help his friend survive Paco quickly taught him how to make hash. He got a few kilos of Kief and ran through a sample batch to show him how it was done. The Shadow was nearly broke from living on the run and needed to make some money. Paco knew that his friend would be able to use the knowledge to hustle and support himself.

It was time for Paco to get back to the states. Before he went back he wanted to spend Easter week in Andalucia when it was possible to hear the Calo Gypsies sing the Ancient primal "Ceuta". He did, and then, after a pleasant week in Lisbon among the "Fado" singers he returned to NY.

One last incident occurred which served to remind Paco that "eternal vigilance is the price of freedom". Paco had not left tangier with anything to smoke. After the London incident he wasn't about to enter the US holding anything.

As he exited baggage control he was approached by a plainclothes US Customs Agent. "What's up"? Said Paco. "Sir we need for you to come with us". The guy had a partner and a baggage cart. So Paco was taken to a small room with a desk and a chair. Sitting down at the desk the partner began to ask questions and write down the answers. "Did anyone give you anything to carry?" Etc. "What's this about" said

Paco. "You look a little bulky to us Mr. Paco" they said. "Do you mind if we search your person" and without waiting for permission began to pat Paco down. He began by feeling Paco's armpits. They were dry as a bone. As he worked his way down the agent looked up and could see that Paco was relaxed and was smiling at him. In that moment the agent knew he was clean. They let him go. But they had been waiting.

CAMBRIDGE 1964

When they were reunited in Cambridge, Paco and Maya were very different people than what they had been before. After they had been through what they self-termed "survival school" life simply couldn't faze them. Reasoning that since they had survived a winter in Tangier then surviving anywhere else should be easier they were they were young, savvy, beautiful, confident and very happy.

They had several issues to address immediately.

1st was a place to live. They stayed for a couple nights at a friends house and Paco went to the storage garage and retrieved the Morris Minor.

They rented a small place above a store on the Somerville line. Paco found a box of cheap plastic siren rings and gave them out to all the neighborhood kids. "Blow them if you see a stranger hanging around" he said.

Each time they left the house they drove around the maze of streets in North Cambridge. They called it "the Cambridge Whirlpool" they would jump in one end and pop out the other. It was impossible for anyone to follow them.

After a week or two they were in a coffeehouse when they saw Detective Gruff. He came over to their table. "How are you guys?" he said. "Piss off Gruff" Said Maya and gave him the finger. "We aren't in Tangier now Gruff" said Paco "were on my home turf now". Maya leaned over the table. "You can tell my father that if he bothers me again with creeps like you he will never hear from me again. Now Piss OFF".

It worked, for that aspect of their lives, at least for the time being. Paco knew that Maya's father loved her. In fact Paco liked her father, and could understand his viewpoint. But the fathers viewpoint wasn't what was important to Maya. Paco respected and defended her independence.

They were still back in the lion's den however

The Fed's wanted the Shadow. They really wanted him badly.

They were making inquiries everywhere.

The Mad Scientist came over one day in an excited state and announced that he had been doing research and had concluded that there was an area around a small town in West Virginia that should contain large amounts of wild pot. He explained that during World War Two the Japanese had occupied Manila. Because the US Navy (and Army) needed hemp to make rope an area ten miles square was planted near one particular town. He concluded with the statement "it was supposed to have been all pulled up after the war." Paco and Maya looked at each other. "They couldn't have got it all" they said. The Mad Scientist agreed.

Since the Feds were so active and they were running low on smoke, they decided it might be a good time to be out of town.

They went to West Virginia. They checked into a Motel with a pool, and drove around the target area for three days. Nothing. There was another plant that looked very much like it but wasn't. After a hundred false alarms they began to wonder. At each sighting they had pulled over and examined "the sighting" and found it wanting. Although it looked like pot it was some other plant.. The false alarm plant acquired the name "3 fingered shit".

For three days they searched all the farms, meadows, back roads, roadside plants and greenery within a 10-mile radius of the target town. They drove and drove and looked and looked. All they saw was "the 3 fingered shit". Deciding to give it up leave in the morning they dropped acid and floated in the swimming pool. All they could see when they closed their eyes was marching fields of "3 fingered shit". In the morning without saying a word to each other they got in the car and drove directly to it. They had passed it a couple days before and it must have registered on their subconscious. By a barn near the road was the real thing. It wasn't a lot perhaps a half-pound, and it wasn't very strong at all. But it was real Cannabis Sativa so they felt vindicated and pronounced the trip a great success.

When they returned word spread quickly of their exploit.

The Fed's had had enough. They began to close in.

The first indication was when every kid in the neighborhood started blowing their siren rings.

The second indication was when Paco's brother came over and said he had had a call from a detective who had been friendly, and said that the police wanted to "interview" him. Paco said "sure" and went down to Cambridge Police Headquarters. Maya went with him and sat quietly on a bench across from a desk by the door to the detective's area.

Inside were several Federal Agents. They told Paco "We
have arrested your friend the Mad Scientist". The lead
Federal Agent went on to explain that they had raided the mad
scientists house and found a couple ounces of the West
Virginia pot and an assortment of other incriminatables.
Given the Mad Scientists record he was in real trouble. Also,
they had information from a "reliable informant" that Paco
was smuggling from Mexico and Europe, and that Boston was
a "Gateway City" and a "Major Marijuana Port".

Paco said "don't be ridiculous" and "Why do you guys care
about a little pot anyway what's wrong with you in the land of
the alleged free."

Maya could hear them talking in the other room the Federal
accusations and Paco's denials. At one point she saw one of
the agents come out and take a green cloth bag with a string
tied top off the table. He took it back in where they were
questioning Paco and she could hear them laying out the
contents and telling Paco he better give up the Shadow if he
wanted to help the Mad Scientist. Paco said, "you know I

can't do that". They started to argue about the "confidential informant" and his information and about smuggling etc. The agent that had taken the green cloth bag in brought it back out and laid it on the desk by the door. He went back to the interrogation.

Maya stood up. There was a patrolman half-asleep at the desk. Walking over to the door she called in "Paco I'm going home now." Then walking out of the detectives area past the lowest paid in the US patrolman she gave him a brilliant smile "Oh", she said, "my purse" and with a quick motion she picked up the green bag and tucked it under her arm. Clutching it under her wing like a clutch bag at a debutante ball she sashayed out of there gently swaying the same body that had stopped traffic in Spain.

The Mad Scientist was released in the morning for "lack of evidence"

Paco however was grilled for another hour. Paco demanded to confront their "confidential informant". "A person has a right to confront their accuser", he said.

"Your going to meet him they said". "I can't wait," said Paco. "Whoever he is he's telling you a pack of lies. Am I under arrest?" asked Paco? Not yet they said. Paco left and went home.

A couple days later, with the Mad Scientist now free, Paco and the Feds went at it again down at Cambridge Police Headquarters. Because Paco was on good terms with a public relations sergeant and knew one of the detectives he felt comfortable being there. In regard to the Federal Officers his stepfather had been one (for the military) and he felt completely comfortable going toe to toe with them. "What do you guys want from me?" he asked them. Actually he liked them. They were for the most part sincere energetic idealistic and bright as shiny buttons. A couple of them were pretty surly but you expect that in a mix. He tried to appeal to their sense of justice. "What crime have these people committed?

How do you acquire jurisdiction when the Constitution only grants the State authority to pass laws that affect the health and welfare of the governed. Pot affected neither. They were Federal Officers sworn to uphold the constitution so what about the principle of equal protection. If cigarettes and liquor were legal how could they in good conscience be a part of enforcing laws against relatively harmless pot?"

These guys were swayed a little and were a little sheepish. Some of them agreed with him and tried to be reasonable. They were typical college guys, just a little uninformed thought Paco.

The leader was a tall polished young man whom Paco later found out was one of Robert Kennedy's Justice Department Special Agents. Agent "Young Turk" expressed sympathy for Paco's viewpoint and suggested Paco should take his views to the legislature. He was really quite friendly. He seemed actually pretty amused by the missing evidence and was treating Paco with great courtesy and respect. He obviously seemed to believe that he meant no harm. "If you are the good guys" Paco challenged "then how come your invading peoples rights?"

Some of the others were Rabid. They trotted out their "confidential informant"

No it wasn't Gruff. They dragged forth a character that looked he was from a Florida moonshine horror show death row picnic. This cracker had orange dyed hair very few teeth and 5 day growth of beard. He looked like a demented speed freak.

Bit by bit the story came out. The "C.I." had laid down his hoe at a Laredo Texas Prison Farm a few weeks before and escaped. A year before, in jail in Texas, for a week, he had been the cellmate of the Shadow. At least he said so. After escaping he had nowhere else to go, he claimed, and had been on the way to Paco's old address when he was arrested by the Cambridge PD. Looking at the guys appearance and the orange dyed hair Paco could believe it. (The getting arrested

part.) The campus police would have notified the Cambridge
PD immediately.

The Cracker had told the Cambridge PD (who immediately
notified the Feds) that he was here to visit a big smuggler
named Paco who was a pal of the Shadows, and wanted to
trade his information (about Paco) in return for his freedom.
He was terrified of being returned to the Texas Justice System
because he was a well known and notorious informer who had
been given the hoe job in return for finking on various other
inmates who would love to get their hands on him.

He had made up an elaborate cock and bull story based on a
few fragments he had heard from the Shadow who always told
stories enhanced to impress. The more he talked about the
details of his accusations the more he was hung by his own
petard. Paco pointed out all the inconsistencies in the guy's
story. He pronounced it total bullshit and defied anyone to
prove a word of it.

It was this crackers appearance that had caused the Mad Scientist to be busted and Paco was pissed. Is this the best you've got, he sneered. To his great credit Agent "Young Turk" intervened. He agreed with Paco. This guys full of shit. He just doesn't want to go back to Texas. Paco was sent home.

The Confidential Informant was sent back to Texas where somebody dropped a concrete block on his head from the third tier.

Paco had had more than enough. Being followed, harassed, falsely accused, was something no one needed. He talked to Maya and after considering their probable future in the Boston area they decided to go to California and "start a new life"

Paco had collected some money from the sale of his inventory and a few other moneys owed to him, and was ready to go, but before he left he wanted one last shot at "The Establishment". He was determined to stage one last "in your face" "Hootenanny".

He applied for a permit from the Hatch Memorial Shell and initially it was routinely approved. A few days later when they found out he was planning to donate the proceeds to Marten Luther Kings activist arm the "Student Nonviolent Coordinating Committee" They canceled the permit.

When Paco heard that the permit was canceled he called a press conference. He accused the City of Boston, and the Metropolitan District Commission, (who had jurisdiction of the Shell) of racism and prejudice. "OK for the rich white kids but not the poor black kids" he thundered.

The newspapers love embarrassing politicians, so it was front-page news. TV and radio covered it too.

Then Paco sent Maya down to the Police Chiefs office in Cambridge to get a "Permit to Block a Sidewalk" good for three days in front of a friends music store in Harvard Square. The evening of the third day was Harvard Commencement in Harvard Stadium.

None of this registered on the Cambridge Police Chief (lowest paid force in the country) who personally issued a gilt-edge bonified certificate of a Permit to Block the Sidewalk for 72 hours to the charming young lady with the brilliant smile in the tight knit dress.

With a couple phone calls and surprising few dollars they ordered a platoon of Police for "Security". Then in the window of their friend's music store they began the performance. They weren't alone. Performers appeared out of the woodwork like magic. First the local people played and then performers started to arrive from out of town. They had called down to NY and put out the word in the coffeehouses and soon the hardcore heroes of the folk world showed up.

Len Chandler flew up from NY and started to hang speakers all over the outside of the building. Len sang many sets and roused the crowd that quickly gathered. The word spread around Harvard Square, that night they made the evening news. Not to be outdone the other stations carried it too. Most of the TV stations also owned Radio Stations so the radio started to carry it. It was a happening. Into the second night musicians were arriving from all over New England. Taj Mahal showed up and played Louie Lou I on a clunky old piano for 22 hours at least. Peter Stampfel and Steve Weber Played at least 12 hours. The longer it went on the more the momentum built. Finally on the third night, Fred Neil and Karen Dalton had the crowd swaying. With the all the major radio stations broadcasting live coverage every 20 minutes the crowd swelled to 35,000 people. In a small side street off Harvard Square that was a lot of people. More than the street could handle. The crowd became a little unruly as only Boston crowds/mobs can. At about that moment Harvard Commencement let out.

 It was utter Chaos.

The Blue Blood upper crust ran smack into Paco's crowd. No body could move. When you added in the crowd trying to leave the Commencement it come to about 50,000 people. The Harvard people just wanted to go through the square and maybe 20 000 people wanted to get into the little side street where the performance was continuing out side now in front of the music store.

Eventually added to the cacophony of honking horns angry voices and folk music came the sound of Sirens. The Entire Cambridge Fire Brigade had been called out to break up the crowd. Slowly inch by inch the wailing fire engines drove through the people and dispersed them.

Maya was photographed and interviewed by all the newspapers and TV crews. She was proud of Paco and with shining eyes told him "I have a whole new level of respect for you, you are a great person."

"Those people will never do another event in my city,' said the Cambridge Police Chief to all the Reporters and Irate Harvard Officials.

"It's Reeeely time to go now" said Paco

One thing happened before they left that was significant.

Paco was in his friends Music store a few days before their departure when he was approached by someone he knew. It was a professor from the University. "Paco", he said. "The Family has become aware of your plans to go across country and would like ask you if you would do something for them." "What family" said Paco. "The Kennedy Family" the Professor said. "What do they want?" Asked Paco. "They want you to stop in Dallas and give them the benefit of you impressions." "How do I do that?" Said Paco. "That's up to you" said the professor.

A few days later Paco and Maya left for California. It felt great to be free, anonymous, in love, happy, and on the road again.

DALLAS TEXAS

The two young people entered Dallas, Texas after a three-day drive from Cambridge Mass. Their names were Paco and Maya. These were not their real name's but having lived "underground" and "on the cheap" in the Spanish Gypsy and Arabic cultures of Andalucia, Algeria, and Morocco they had adopted the gypsy life style and used other names routinely as a way of confusing their trail. Maya didn't want her parents catching up to her. (They had threatened Paco with guns.) And Paco didn't want the Justice Department agents who were looking for some of his friends to get too close.

It seemed like, after the JFK Assassination, the Fed's just had no sense of humor. Neither did anybody else, especially Maya's father. Maya had briefly visited her parents in NY upon her return from North Africa, and although her gun-toting father was completely astounded by her presence, poise, confidence, and resourcefulness, he was still determined to "rescue her".

For Paco and Maya It was common to adopt street names while traveling, and an occasional change of identity prevented parking tickets, bills, bounced grocery store, garage and electric company checks, traffic citations, process servers, Fed's, parents, and other unpleasentries from showing up at their door. They often communicated in front of outsiders (Payos) in a mixture of Spanish, a few words of Sanskrit, Hipster English, Arabic sign language, and prearranged signals. No one had a clue what was being said when they talked to each other. It came in very handy.

The weather had been good for the drive and only two incidents occurred on the drive to cause ripples in their tranquil passage. One had been in Oklahoma, where they had stopped at what had been advertised on billboards for at least a hundred miles as the "cheapest gas station in the state". They were surprised to find out that someone Paco knew ran it. It was a Choctaw Indian that had befriended Paco on one of his teenage hitchhiking trips when he had been a kid. They had a brief reunion, small world etc., then had proceeded.

The second incident was a little more disconcerting. It was about one in the morning when they crossed the Texas Border. Making a pit stop in a small corner gas station next to the highway Maya, who was an incredibly beautiful and exotic woman with an unbelievable figure, was spotted coming out of the ladies room by a group of drunk yahoo's in a pickup truck. It was apparent that they had never seen what appeared to be a stunning young Spanish Gypsy woman. Maya was wearing what was, for her, normal attire, but what must have appeared to be an exotic dancer costume to the testosterone infested eeeehaaaa and yaaahoooo load of horny young crackers in the truck.

Maya was behind the wheel as the tiny Morris Minor (the "Marvelous Morris, Mechanical Marvel of the Modern Mechanized Machine Age") pulled out onto the interstate. The truck pulled out after them. The Morris was reasonably fast with a top cruising speed of 65 and got nearly 90 miles to a gallon on flat terrain in overdrive. The highway was dark and empty a few miles from the small town as the truck hurtled up from the rear and came alongside.

Whooping and hollering the 3 guys in the cab and the four in the bed 1st drove along side then in front of and then behind and then got in front and slowed down. Paco was sure that so far from any kind of help with that many guys there could be a problem. Could be? Shit they Had a problem. Slowing the Morris, speeding up, slowing almost to a stop then pulling away didn't work. This went on for several nerve-racking minutes. By changing speed, almost stopping then accelerating they managed to keep 30 feet or so away from the truck.   Paco told Maya to pull off on the right shoulder. They had done this already a couple times and then pulled away when the truck stopped just ahead and on the left shoulder

This time Paco opened his side door and with a tire iron fished from under the seat pointed it over the doorframe as though it was the barrel of a rifle. In the spilled light on the dark

highway he hoped it would cause the guys to hesitate. Paco
had some really good Karate training (his brother taught at a
marshal arts school frequented by various Federal Agencies).
But as a talented midlevel adept he knew that despite many
successful encounters in the barrios, casbah's and medinas of
Algeria and Morocco he would easily be overpowered by this
large a number of beer-fueled healthy Americans.

He wished for Mayas sake that he had a knife and had often
carried a wicked one in the past when hitchhiking cross-
country in his early teens. It had proven essential for defense
against child molesters, perverts, and other serial undesirables
bent on molestation of one sort or another. As a 26-year-old
adult, student, businessman, and folkloric instrumentalist he
hadn't carried a knife in years. On other previous cross
country trips he had carried an old 32 caliber starters pistol
which was legal, looked real and made a great "warning shot"
noise. It too had occasionally proved useful, but it was lost in
time, drifted off to the world of lost tools and socks. After a
quite momentary pause with the little Morris on the right
shoulder of the deserted highway and the truck idling a dozen

yards ahead on the opposite shoulder the passenger door of the truck opened and a large tall redneck emerged.

"What's up?" Called Paco, "what do you want?" He saw the big guy jerk back with shock as he heard the male voice. It was then that Paco realized the guys thought they had been chasing down some "Yankee poon-tang" they must have seen the Mass Plates, and with Paco's long hair assumed it was two woman traveling together. Certainly their attention had been focused on Maya. Encouraged by the big guy's hesitation Paco called again "what do you want with us?" While pretending to aim the tire iron he lifted his head up and then sighted down the tire iron as though he were trying to achieve a better "sight picture". He could here other voices in the truck talking now to each other the but the only one out of the truck was the big guy who was still hesitating, not willing to step into the pool of light created by the Morris headlights.

Tipping the uncertainty into a new reality Paco called out in a pretty good imitation of the local dialect "Y'all have a good night now heah? We don't want no trouble". Paco could hear the other voices more intently talking now and then to his immense relief the big guy got back in the truck. The truck made a U-turn and they drove off back towards the town.

 Arriving in Dallas later on a late October day in 1964 it was bright and sunny. The reason for the stopover was threefold. It provided a convenient break and rest stop on their drive to the West Coast. Maya had an old school friend to visit, and Paco had been asked by a friend of the Kennedy family who had become aware of their travel plans to stop in Dallas and "gather his impressions", and to "provide them with the benefit of his viewpoint". How he should accomplish the latter was of course up to him.

They stayed with Maya's school friend the first night and in the morning began the search for a place to stay. At that time in Dallas because of a surplus of oil money seeking an investment outlet it was common to see empty apartments in brand new buildings with a pool, new carpet and drapes, for 125 dollars a month or less.

Checking the papers and looking all day while familiarizing themselves with the layout of the city they liked the new places but on their low budget, and because Paco was intent on "gathering his impressions". They settled on a large room rented by the week for 14 dollars a block or so from Lee Harvey Oswald's former address. It was well situated as a base, giving a feel for Oswald's life style and neighborhood, his poverty, and hopefully insights into his thought process. By studying the peers of an individual Paco hoped to get inside Oswald's head. If even just on a neighborhood level. For example Oswald couldn't have had much money, if he did he would have lived in a better place. They were certainly available cheaply enough. It led Paco to the conclusion that Oswald was sincere in his economic difficulties, and probably was easily manipulated because of it.

Paco's next move was to make a list of every nightclub, private club, restaurant, dance hall and honky-tonk within 10 miles of Dallas. It took a week or more to cold canvass and audition at every single one. His reasoning was that A. by visiting every spectrum of the local "scene" he would get a feel for the community. B. He could rely on the fact that Texans were proud of their good relations with the members of their Mexican community. C. Texans would be unable to tell the difference between Mexican and Spanish music. (Since they both sounded Spanish) and the beautiful Flamenco being extremely rare in the local cultural environment would have a certain entertainment "shock value".

Maya was all for it. She enjoyed going out, dressing up, and being admired. Paco had been to Dallas before. He had stayed there a few days when he was 14 years old and hitchhiking across the US. In the 50's phone calls were still a nickel in Dallas. Reluctant to hitch through the southwestern deserts, he had made a deal with a drive-away agency to be back up driver on a delivery run to LA. He had lied about his age and driving experience and traded a camera to the primary driver for the ride. He had also been through Dallas several times a couple years before on business and had some idea of the layout of the city.

It was serendipitous that their first night out on this project happened to be Halloween. Because they had been traveling they had not paid attention to the calendar and were blissfully unaware as they unpacked and dressed to go out for the evening of cold canvass auditions that this night was different from any other ordinary evening. Living in Spain and North Africa both Paco and Maya had, without thinking about it picked up some unusual fashion proclivities. Paco wore his usual short boots, jeans, and flowing polka dot shirt and rimless grandpa glasses. Maya's skill with makeup was extraordinary. She could create many different personas with her makeup-case/paintbox. This evening she created a mask of sensual beauty, and donned a soft thin North African Jellaba (her favorite article of clothing). It flowed over her body like a erotic monk's robe and allowed her beautiful face to turn and emerge from the hooded cowling like a framed painting. The "shock value" was enormous. So it was that they ventured forth.

They had decided to start upscale and work their way down. So the first stop was a large private club on the edge of the city. It looked busy and crowded and when the door opened several heads appeared around the door frame to peer at the new arrivals there were squeals of delight and a hostess rushed forward to grab them by the hand and gushed "your sure to win"! Pleased by the attention and welcome but confused Paco exchanged glances with Maya and asked "win what". "The prize" said the lady, and several others gathered around the door to watch the new arrivals concurred. "The prize for best costume" the nice lady said and with a bobbing of heads all the others again chorused their agreement. Paco and Maya looked at each other and started to laugh.

He turned to the hostess and said "but this is the way we dress every day". It was then that he realized that all the others were in some sort of costume or another. Bit by bit they explained they were not members, or guests, and they were not in costume. In fact he was a musician looking for work and wanted to audition. The crowd by the door shrieked with delight when it was explained. "They dress like this every day" went around the place in a flash and many more crowded to see. Maya loved it. "Yes he could play" and they immediately arranged for him to get up on their small stage. It was a good set and created a nice peaceful moment in the place.

The members of the audience seemed to really like it but when they found where he and Maya were from several people spontaneously blurted "we didn't do it". Paco asked "didn't do what" and was surprised that they were referring to the Kennedy Assassination. Curious, did that mean that it was common knowledge locally that someone else had? Even more curious, they received exactly the same reception at the next 3 or 4 clubs they visited that night including the part with "we didn't do it" when they heard where they were from.

They visited most of the outlying and upscale private country clubs that evening and they were all having Halloween Parties. Paco played at most and was well received. His theory that Texans would like the Flamenco was proving to be completely true. He and Maya went home in the wee hours laughing insanely over "this is what we wear every day" and reflecting more soberly on "we didn't do it".

Over the course of the next week, they visited every possible venue working from the outside of the city in toward the center of Dallas. This process included most of the large restaurants. In the case of the restaurants appointments, usually in the afternoon, had to be made for auditions to play for the owners, managers, ostensibly to try to create a job playing certain dinner hours etc. The music was well received. But no employment ensued. Paco reasoned that it was true that he and Maya were pretty bizarre for an upscale restaurant. They were fed and appreciated, however, and still heard that recurring theme of "we didn't do it" when they were asked where they were from.

It was on a Friday night that they went to downtown Dallas to apply for work at the nightspots and clubs in Jack Ruby's old neighborhood. Ruby's Club was closed but there were others wide open up and down the same street with booze, bands, broads, and an occasional stripper as part of the show. One place had a packed house in a big second floor bar. It was a traditional Dallas Nightclub and was a wild place.

Paco asked to audition for a gig, and they put him on between the band and the stripper. The response was amazing. They whooped hollered, cheered.

It reminded Paco of what a local prosecutor had told him a few years before when he had come down from Boston to bail out the Shadow who had run afoul of the Texas justice system. When asked if the friends skin color would work against him, the prosecutor had leaned back in his chair and had said "helllll no. Dowwn heah in Takesass we git along with our niggers and spicks jus fine."

Oddly enough that philosophy was reflected in the cheering and applause that night. They had never heard real Spanish music before but saw it as a celebration of their culture and Texas heritage and just loved it. The management passed a hat and collected a hat full of money from which they deftly removed some of the larger bills muttering something about a house cut. Paco was invited to come back the following night and play on a popular prime time radio show that was broadcast directly from the club. The owner told Paco he was hired as a regular part of the entertainment (his pay to come from the hat) That him and his pretty missus were welcome. Beaming with pleasure at the responses from his customers "Yooooo Lee-Roy y'all got yo self a reeel gee tar picker roun heah now!" he was completely sincere.

Maya got along great with the strippers and waitresses, they made friends with one of the strippers and some of the band members. For her it was fun going out to this packed club and enjoyed her status as muse to the music. She dressed up in various costumes and had a lot of fun. The only drawback for her was the danger of being injured by the flying bodies, chairs, tables, bottles and glass that would fly when the fights broke out. Fights broke out regularly. If not one a night then two every other night. One night instead of the conventional flurry of hard thuds, excited voices, and crashing furniture there was an interesting incident.

 Apparently a huge six and a half foot Texan (they breed them down there) leaned over and said something to a tall beautiful woman sitting at a stageside table. Her companion, who was a three and half foot dwarf resented the intrusion and said so. Something like "get lost shorty" was said. What happened next amazed Paco. The dwarf jumped up onto the table bringing himself to the same height as the big guy, and hit him hard with a long armed round house right on the side of his head reeling the big man back. Jumping onto the next table the dwarf did it again. Each swing drove the big guy stumbling across the club as the dwarf jumped from tabletop to tabletop driving his opponent towards the top of the stairs by the exit. The place was packed as usual on a weekend night so the crowd had to move out of the way in panic.

The Management had long since erected a metal grill work barrier that the employees could take shelter behind when these things happened. Paco who had been about to go on stage passed his fragile guitar to Maya who was safe behind the barrier, and was pressed against the wall by the crush of people. It was over in a moment. The regular bouncers lifted the inert form of the now comatose Texan and dragged him down the stairs, heels bumping on the many steps. In the momentary silence following the violence the thump thump of the exiting cowboys heels was like the heartbeat of Dallas.

It was for sure that this was a bad-ass mainline hardcore Dallas nightclub just a few blocks from Dealey Plaza similar to and located near Ruby's now defunct Carousel Club. The owner and his cronies were all friends of Ruby and had similar "business interests". This was a rough bunch, the fights were just indicative of the mindset. Guns were bought and sold, everybody carried one. One night at the bar he saw the owner, a huge round bullet headed individual called "Lee-Roy" threatened to disfigure a gorgeous call girl with glittering sausage knife. Packets of powder were passed, and money changed hands. Paco saw all this out of the corner of his eye as he waited to play, watched the show, or from his unique vantage point of onstage.

"You know a man by who he walks with" (Old Spanish proverb) So If this is what Ruby's friends are, then what was he, mused Paco. A couple weeks of this went by.

Shopping in the same corner grocery store that Oswald had probably shopped in and walking around the neighborhood they soaked up the vibes. These people were poor, bored, and not very bright. What was interesting was that Oswald had fit right in.

Paco and Maya were not fitting in so well. Perverts were constantly trying to touch Maya when they were shopping. On a couple occasions Cadillac's had pulled up along side them, usually at a red light, as they drove downtown to the Club from the heights. The passenger would brandish a pistol and then would drive off. Paco and Maya figured it was the Mass. Plates and the foreign Car. One night a big car pulled up beside them at a light and the passenger rolled down his window. Waving a pistol he shouted "diiid Yew alll heah whut ahhh saaid?" Nonplussed Paco said "no", staring at the pistol wondering what would happen next "Gottdam good thang too" said the passenger in the other car and the car pulled away. Paco pulled over a few blocks further on and tried to tell a Dallas patrol car that someone had just threatened them with a gun. The officer had looked them up and down and said "that's what you git round heah" and drove away.

When they drove a black band member friend home from the club a patrol car would follow them through the neighborhood a few feet behind their bumper and then peel away. Paco and Maya figured they were attracted to the foreign car and mixed racial passengers. Although they weren't stopped they found it unnerving and so they aborted a small bag of pot through a hole in the floor that was expressly for that purpose. Paco had installed it a few years before figuring (correctly) that a closely following police car would never see a small baggie (or the contents thereof) emerging from underneath the car.

On a Friday night Paco was standing near the second floor entrance when emerging from the staircase came two US Federal Agents. It was Special Agent Young Turk and his partner. Paco knew both of them because they had interviewed him at some length the previous year in Boston. After "the Shadow" had jumped bail and fled the country they had their bowels in a downroar to find him but they had to respect that Paco would never cooperate in giving up a friend.

 But that isn't why two of Former Attorney General Robert Kennedy's Justice Department Agents were standing in the doorway of a Dallas Nightclub on a Friday night in November 1964. A year after the fact someone had got the bright idea of investigating Jack Ruby's peer group as a way of making judgements and assumptions about him. The bad part about this was that they looked like what they were; bright young idealistic Federal Agents with suits and ties to match. The worst part, as it turned out, was that they knew Paco by his real name and said ****** what are you doing here? Shhh said Paco I Work here. They were pretty stunned, Paco had gotten away with quite a bit in their opinion but he amused and amazed them with his ability to disappear from their radar screen at will

The Fed's had a grudging respect for Paco. In addition to the "missing green evidence bag incident" the year before they had been listening on his tapped phone line when he called coffee houses all over the country and had offered a "pound of pot reward" for a transient who had stolen some money from his import business. The Fed's had been amazed when "the Walkaway Kid" had called into collect the reward from the opposite coast where he had retrieved Paco's money at gunpoint. Paco was loyal to his friends, and had raised money for Children's Hospital in addition to SNCC.

He obviously meant no harm, was well regarded by the younger Kennedy Brothers, and didn't commit any serious crimes. Trying to adapt, Special Agent Young Turk incredulously whispered "you mean you are in place"? "I have been working here a few weeks" said Paco. At that moment the Maitre de stepped up and escorted them to a table. As she did so Paco noticed the doorman, who was chief henchman to the owner looking at him strangely. Over the rest of the weekend things seemed normal. He didn't see the Fed's again. But he did notice the doorman watching him.

Sunday and Monday the Club was closed. On the following Tuesday in the late afternoon Paco drove downtown to see if could get the owner to give him a small steady salary. If he were going to stay longer he would need the money. He liked doing the radio show and was having fun performing, the environment not withstanding. As he climbed the long flight of stairs the upper entrance door was wedged open.

With the lower door closed the empty the stairwell collected the sound from above like a giant ear. He could hear the owner and his head honcho talking all the way from the back office as clear as a bell. He paused for a breath on the long staircase and as he leaned against the banister he could hear the voices drifting down from out of sight above.

He heard the honcho say "Lee-Roy ahh bin meanin to tawk to yew about thet git tahh player". Lee-Roy, said "heyyyy don't bother me about thet gee tar player, he bringin in a lotta bizness. Folks like how he play." "But Lee-Roy" the honcho said "That ain't no gee tar player, thet's a git tahhh player". Since they were talking about him Paco listened closely, frozen motionless in the stairwell. "I toll you to leave me alone about thet gee tar player" said Lee-Roy. "That's wut ahm tryin to tell you Lee-roy" said the honcho "thet ain no gee tarrrr player thet's a git ahhhh player." "ohhhhhh" said Lee-Roy, the reference to the Harvard ahhhh penetrating at last. "You probably right, I tell you what, you play it cool and next weekend we'll invite him and that hot woman of his out to the Motel, play a little game of shuffle broad and fix his ass."

Holding his breath Paco quietly retreated down the stairs and eased the door open. It only took a few minutes to drive back to where they had been staying. He walked in the door and saw that Maya was sitting by the bay window sewing. Holding a finger to his lips for silence he gently slapped the back of his left wrist with the four fingers of his right hand. Quickly lifting the index finger in an upward motion he gave the Arabic hand sign for "leave". He repeated the hand sign twice more. Any signal repeated three times meant "urgent". Without a word they packed their bags, packed the car, and were past the city limits on the highway out of town less than 30 minutes later. They pulled over for a moment to adjust a couple of hastily packed things in the car. Before getting back in Paco paused and looked back at the city of Dallas. There had been a shower and there was a huge rainbow over the entire city running north to south. How ironic thought Paco as he and Maya literally drove off into the sunset. One final though occurred to Paco as they drove away.

No one at that Club for the entire 3 weeks had said, "we didn't do it".

BERKELY

After driving through the southwestern deserts, Paco and Maya arrived in San Diego and paused for a few hours at the beach. Maya had never been to California so Paco decided to show her the whole coast. They were tired and cramped from the trip (the Morris was fun but really small.) They had stopped at motels in the desert, but wanted to settle in and rest. Turning north they drove along the water through LA, Malibu, Santa Barbara, Big Sur, finally arriving at Monterey Bay. Paco had lived in SF and knew the area well. On weekends he had often driven an old Jag down the coast road and enjoyed the flower farms, and great ocean views.

On the northern side of the bay was the small retirement community of Pacific Grove.

They found a furnished one room cabin for rent in an off season motel complex near the beach by the entrance to 17 mile drive with a kitchen and bath. Maya got a job in a retail clothing store, and Paco got a commission instrument sales job at a music store. After some rest and regular food (paella, fresh vegetables, cheeseburgers, shrimp curry, steak and chocolate pudding cake.) they explored Monterey County. Some of the large farms in the small town's inland specialized in growing miles of flowers. They drove around the beautiful mountains near Santa Cruz. And spent happy hours on Cannery Row.

They loved to watch the winter storms blow 25 and 30-foot waves ashore in the small inlets near their cabin. Stacked up behind each other, curling their tops above the high wall of water the power of the towering monsters was awesome to watch. Their jobs didn't pay much at all but they were safe, anonymous, and very happy. There were horses for rent at a nearby stable and a couple of times they rented them and rode along the beach on the sunny days. Every evening they would play Honeymoon Bridge. The loser had to take their clothes off first and then they would slowly and thoroughly make love.

It was particularly chilly and rainy that year near the coast and since they hadn't had anything to smoke for a few months, they decided one weekend to drive up to Berkley. They liked Pacific Grove, and Monterey, The peace and quiet, awesome primal beauty, and laid back pace was great but they missed the music scene that they had left behind in Boston. For years there had been an underworld of musicians and transients based out of the coffeehouses in Boston and Cambridge. Mostly centered around the campuses of Boston University, MIT, and Harvard University there was a thriving gypsy-like subculture of music, pot, and politics that included a wide cross section of folksingers, talented dropouts, and various characters in a constantly changing scene.

There was a West Coast version of the same music scene based around University of California at Berkeley. Also they had musician friends and other people they knew from Boston/Cambridge that were currently living in the bay area.

Driving up the inland highway to Berkley they picked up a hitchhiker who by serendipitous good fortune had a small thin joint of excellent pot pinned to the inside of his undershirt. It was a great moment in one sense. After living alone for months outside their usual (however bizarre) social rubric they were back inside the bubble of their pot/drug oriented social peer group.

So much for the peaceful life by the ocean near Monterey Bay. Upon arriving in Berkeley they found friends living in a communal house, and it was a few days before they returned to Pacific Grove. Paco had located an old friend who had also studied Flamenco in Spain and they spent the next weekend at his house in the rain forests north of Marin County.

Living in their Cabin in Monterey now seemed so far from the friends and activities they enjoyed their life began to become a little less idyllic. The trips to Berkeley and Marin County became more frequent and more extended. Finally, they packed the car and moved up to a room in the communal house in Berkeley.

Money was tight since they were now unemployed. For the first week or so Maya saved the day by going out each night for a few potatoes, and shoplifting a couple large steaks . She was good at it and completely disarmed the young male nightshift checkout clerks.

Paco made friends with a Hells Angel, and was invited to ride down to Mexico to burn the crops of a farmer who had been informing. Although he didn't go he got access to kilo bricks of good Mexican pot for $75.00.

This helped the cash flow a lot, not a whole lot because they were sending them East for $200.00 each to friends in Boston. By the time they collected the $125 dollar profit, minus postage, it was usually two weeks, but living communally in 1963, it was enough.

They shared the rent on the 1st floor of a large house with two other couples. They had hot chocolate in the coffee houses, played pool, went to the foreign film theatre on Telegraph Avenue, listened to Joan Baez on the steps of Sproud Hall, ate student food, and settled in to spend the rest of the winter.

Paco had lived a few years before in North Beach, San Francisco and the scene had been hopping. Ron rice was making movies with Eric Nord, City lights bookstore was selling Allen Ginsburg's Howl, Lawrence Ferlenghetti and Bob Kaufman were reading poetry in the brawling Grant Avenue Bagel Shop where Paco's brother had been a bartender.

Things were fine for a while, Paco started to do a few gigs over in North Beach at the Coffee Gallery. It was a great moment for Paco on the spiritual level. When Paco had previously lived on Grant Ave he had regularly heard the "Maestro of Comedy" Richard "Lord" Buckley perform "The Nazz", and "Jonah and the Whale". Always beginning with "M'lords and M'ladys of the royal court" Lord Buckley would deliver his message of love and humor. He always broke everybody up.

It was Lord Buckley who had dubbed Paco "Prince Paco" in 1960. In the beatnik world it was like getting kissed by the

Pope. Playing on the same stage as his mentor made Paco
feel like he had arrived somewhere with his music. He was
gaining confidence as a performer. Inspired by Maya in the
audience he created some beautiful pieces expressing the
passion of his North Beach memories and played his fusion of
Flamenco and Folk. He created special moments suspended in
time, which were surprisingly well received.

They had a stable month or so but then two friends arrived
from Cambridge. It was the Mad Scientist and the Sidekick.
They had been through a harrowing trip. They left Boston
shortly after Paco and Maya but while driving through Texas
they had been pulled over basically because they were a mix
racial pair of guys. In the routine (for Texas) search of their
vehicle the trunk was opened. For some reason known only to
themselves one of the guys had thrown several "fingers" of
Hashish randomly around the trunk. "What's thet" said the
trooper "looks lahke dog sheit to me". It didn't smell like
dog shit, so the upshot was that they had been arrested,
quickly convicted and given 15 years each in a Texas
Penitentiary.

"Christ, that's awful", said Paco, "how did you get out". "A radio talk show preacher" was the answer, "we wrote to him and told him how his preaching had changed our lives and brought redemption to us in our prison cells, and if he would only go the bond for our release pending an appeal, we would testify at his church and on the radio about how we had been saaaaaaved!. We had been in for two months before he came down to see us and agreed to go our appeal bond." "What did you say to him to get him to go your bond?" Maya asked? The chorused reply: "Jesus, Jesus, get me out of here, Jesus Jesus Jesus, get me out of here, Jesus Jesus Jesus Jesus, get me out of here." Paco was incredulous, "and that worked?" "Yup, plus he gave us some expense money and got our car out of impound."

"But what about the appeal and the State of Texas?" asked Maya. "We can never go back", said one, "we changed our identity's anyway" said the other, who had already adopted the identity of a podiatrist from Pennsylvania and was last seen practicing in Santa Barbara giving rich ladies foot massages. Upon receiving their car from the Texas impound lot they discovered that the troopers had not found their stash of Sandoz LSD.

So instead of heading to the preachers church to "testify" about how they had been saved and all they headed for Las Vegas to see if they could manipulate the dice at craps while "under the influence" so to speak.

This plan was actually going fairly well until the casino management decided that they didn't know what these guys were on but it must be something and threw them out. Hence their arrival in Berkeley a few days later.

Coincidental with the arrival of their friends, the tempo of drug activities picked up dramatically.

1st of all, their two friends from Boston had about a hundred or more doses of pure Sandoz LSD. Tucked in the corner of an envelope the little packet of undiluted powder was smaller than a postage stamp. The method of measuring out doses was to use a hypodermic of a very specific small diameter, and after diluting the powder with a very specific amount of distilled water, to drip say five tiny drops on a sugar cube. On one previous occasion while rushing to an airport a friend had been measuring out doses in a car. The friend unable to cope with the preciseness of the procedure had simply sprayed the top layer of the box of sugar cubes. The dosages varied widely.

It was couple of these cubes that had remained unnoticed in the glove compartment of the two guys from Boston when they had been pulled over in Texas, and which they had later taken in Vegas. With the unknown dosage no wonder they thought they could manipulate the dice. The thing that Paco wondered was that since we create our own realities; could they have?

Anyway the 100 precisly measured cubes were sold immediately by the two guys to the Berkeley fringe community. There was a talented biochemist who was turning out some pretty good refined Lysergic Acid Dythalimide, in Berkley at the time, but the Top end Swiss

Lab produced Sandoz LSD 25 (the popular belief was that the 25 was the number of purification steps it had been through.) was on another level entirely. No physical side effects whatsoever. Introducing the high end Acid had two effects. It attracted lots of other drugs, and although it conveyed a certain status, it attracted attention, the wrong kind.

They had their first break-in, Paco saw one of the robbers leaving and told the victim of the theft who he had seen. Later the same individual would offer Paco a lift and make an unsuccessful attempt to shove Paco out of the moving vehicle into oncoming traffic. The martial arts training was really coming in handy. What with meth freaks, snuff freaks, and animal sacrifice Satan freaks, California can be a rough place.

About that same time some amphetamine showed up along with some methadrine, followed by some genial gentlemen from Oakland with free samples of, were they ready? Heroin. Added to this mix in what was now becoming a crowded house, there was a new hallucinogenic that was still legal, at least for a few more weeks.(The legislation was rapidly going forward but it hadn't passed yet.)

DMT or Dimethaltriptamine was smoked on tealeaves and gave a twenty minute intense hallucinogenic experience. On a phone call back east another crony of Paco's offered to mail a large "economic relief" package of it out west before it became illegal. The house was quickly becoming the psychedelic headquarters of the Bay Area. US Federal Agents were active in the community.

The Lab's were often raided, and one night Paco went to the back door to find the most famous underground maker of LSD standing on the dark porch with two huge chemical bottles, one in each arm. He was panting and had been running. "Can you keep these cold for me? They have to stay in the fridge. I will give you something good later if you help me out". Paco had done several small trades with the "chemist" and felt comfortable in saying "sure". The two tall huge blue bottles stayed there for two weeks before they were retrieved. Maya said "it probably represented the entire California LSD supply".

The "chemist" (actually a brilliant and talented biochemist) was eventually apprehended but not before he converted those two huge bottles of raw lysergic into a couple million doses of excellent nearly perfect LSD. Paco was rewarded with maybe a couple hundred doses in powder form. He traded a few for some pot but then carefully sealed, stored and stashed the rest. It would come in really handy later.

Each day they had gone to the post office waiting for the "economic relief bundle" from back east. For several days there was no package at "general delivery" but one afternoon as they climbed the stairs to the Berkeley Post Office. They noticed a powerful and pervasive odor emanating from the building. "Its here" they said, and so it was. The stench inside the Post Office was unbelievable and to their amazement the clerk handed over the package holding it by the corner only and keeping it as far as possible from her.

Considering the awesome stench they were a little surprised it had come through, but after all it was technically still legal. (The legislation had been passed but had not been signed yet). The "dose" was approximately a quarter teaspoon of sprayed tealeaves smoked in a pipe. The market value was 3 dollars a dose. After watching a few people experiment with it Paco concluded that it did not look like fun or something he wanted to do and decided not to try it. Maya agreed.

The demand however was unprecedented. One musician who was aware that this was the only DMT in all of California loved it and was determined to "corner the market." He offered a dollar a "dose" for the entire lot. Maya and Paco stayed up all night with quarter teaspoon measure and some tinfoil and next day they traded 1000 small tinfoil packets for $1000.00 in cash.

What with the speed, smack, acid, pot, and closing circle of inevitable "heat" it was time to go.

Paco had been experiencing some ulcerating bleeding, as a result of left over effects from the Tangier dysentery. A local Dr. had suggested that living on the beach in Mexico, eating natural food and smoking a little pot was good for stress related illnesses. His advice was that Paco should give his body a chance to rest and heal.

Just before they left the Bay area Maya was driving the Morris when it was totaled in an intersection accident. She was OK but the car was history.

They bought a well used Oldsmobile hard top convertible with a zillion miles on it for 100 dollars, packed their stuff in and with their now substantial (for them) nest egg, Mayas fluent command of Spanish, an out of date guide book, (Mexico on 5 dollars a day) and their very low to the ground Oldsmobile hardtop they headed for the border stopping to puke every hour for the first three days as they shed the drugs from their systems.

After about 3 days they were clean and happy as they crossed the huge northern Mexican Sonora Desert singing along at the top of their lungs to the Beetle tune. Sommme Dayyy youlll know, I was the one but tomooorrow may rain so I'llll follow the sun. It felt great to be clean, healthy, free, anonymous, solvent, happy and on the road again.

ROAD TO MARSCOTA

Crossing the border had been effortless. Stopping at a Notary public on the US side they had both sworn they were who they said they were. For 2 dollars each they had been issued a Notarized Certificate not that they were who they said they were but that they had solemnly sworn that they were who they said they were. At the time the distinction between the Affirmation and the Oath was lost on the Mexican Immigration authorities. And so, six-month Visas were duly issued to Mr. and Mrs. Hokum Lutchmuck. It matched the name they had given when they bought the Oldsmobile.

It was usual to pass through various inspection stations in the "buffer zone" below the border and they had been through several. A hundred miles or so below the border there were orange cones in the road indicating their lane was to pull over and a crude sign said "Inspection". When they pulled up there were only two very shaggy looking "Pistoleros" with holstered revolvers. The two characters who peered into their car were not Mexican Federals.

They were Bandits. Their lack of any uniform and the crude sign was one tip-off that the stop might not be entirely kosher. Another was the deep furrows on their faces running up their cheeks and across their skulls. Paco realized that he had never seen bullet creases before. It must be an occupational hazard of being a gunfighter. Since these two guys were still here he figured whomever they had been shooting it out with must look a lot worse.

As they circled the car and peered in the windows, Maya seized the initiative. "Oh", she said in Spanish with her perfect Castilian accent, treating them as though they were proper immigration officers. "You must want to see our Visas".

The two denizens looked at each other and figured that made sense and pretended to look at the papers that were thrust into their hands. Paco noticed his visa was being "read" upside down. There was nothing of any value in sight anywhere in the old car, and Paco and Maya certainly looked poor enough. The banditos seemed unsure of themselves for a second. Maya said "Muchos Gracias por su inspection senors" and reached to take the visa's back. Shrugging, the classic desperado with the most scars handed them back, bowed deeply and said "Buenos dias Senora". Exhaling the breath he had been holding Paco pulled away.

It was the next day that they ran into a more serious problem. Now several hundred miles below the border nothing in Paco's previous experience prepared him for what happened next. It was his first journey into the interior of Mexico by car and perhaps because they were so euphorically happy he just wasn't cautious enough. They had pulled off the highway at a lean to restaurant with a chalkboard and some chickens out front 20 miles from the nearest town just to get two bottles of Fanta Naranja (orange soda).

They had been standing by the cooler in the shade for a moment to stretch their legs and neither one of them saw what the old man in the tattered hat did outside. Although Paco kept an eye on the car he never saw the old man carefully drag out a rock and carefully position it in the exit driveway. The activity registered on his peripheral vision but didn't draw his attention. More than 20 feet away and exactly the color of the sandy background the rock was a foot square on the bottom, it weighed at least 30 pounds and had a unique feature. A sharp chisel like finger on top that was carefully angled in the direction of the Oldsmobile's oil pan. Looking at it head-on it couldn't be seen.

As they pulled out they never saw it coming. The good news was that it somehow missed the oil pan. The bad news was that it punctured the transmission pan and broke the internal gear selector lever. They were "dead in the water". It took the rest of the day to shove the car to a parking spot, get it up on blocks, get under it, remove the pan and diagnose the problem. They rented the only available accommodation, which was a room with out a lock on the door in the ramshackle house of the storeowner.

The next day Paco went 20 miles to the nearest town prepared to spend hundreds of dollars to try and get another transmission, or at least another gear selector lever. (They could hammer the pan back into shape and repair it with solder). On the second day Paco finally found a little shop on a side street where tht master machinist said "no problema" and taking his old broken part had welded beads of metal onto it slowly bringing it back to a semblance of the shape of the original. In a matter of minutes using grinding wheels and files the "maestro" produced en exact replica of the original. "Will it work?" asked Paco. "Si comono" (how could it not) was the answer. "Es el mismo" (it's the same). The cost was 50 pesos. Paco bought solder and a cheap propane torch (to repair the pan with) and headed back.

Maya, in the meantime, was not faring as well. Each time she left the room unguarded something else was missing either clothing or jewelry. Because of her command of the language she had befriended the few other souls near where they had broken and it was from them that she learned that the damage to their car had been deliberate and what the old man had done. Many others had been stopped and usually left to get help leaving their possessions to be plundered. In Mayas case, she was told they would be robbed until nothing was left. Then they would have to leave.

Just then Paco arrived with the part and in a couple hours they were gone. Maya was angry though, the young girl of the family had gotten a piece of jewelry with intrinsic value. They quickly recovered their high spirits and roared into Guadalajara (the muffler was getting a little loose) with their guidebook (Mexico on 5 dollars a day) clutched in their hands. They put the car in for service at a shop and checked into a big old Hotel with large high ceilinged 18th century rooms. It had been a long trip but after dinner and some terrific sex, Paco felt rejuvenated. " How bout I go get us something to smoke?" he asked. "Be careful," Maya said.

Exiting the Hotel Paco didn't have to stroll far before he was predictably approached by a "street hustler". "You want a girl?" He was asked. "No but I could use a little mota" (pot) Paco answered. "Yes, yes, I can get" his new pal said. A couple years earlier In Mexico D.F. Paco occasionally might have bought a couple joints from a street hustler like this and that would have been it. But, after the Tangier experience, he knew what would happen when he said to the tout "Actually I want to buy a lot of pot, I want to smuggle it back to the United States in my car. Can you help me with that?"

The hustler's eyes lit up, gleaming with Peso signs. "Si senor, sin problema I can take care of everything for you. I know just the man you need to talk to". Then the hustler had taken Paco directly to a police officials house. Paco knew this would happen because that's what would have happened to anyone, who would have said what he did to a street hustler, excuse me, "tour guide" in the casbah of Tangier. He figured Guadalajara wouldn't be much different. Sure enough the police official woke up and greeted Paco and his "guide". Paco wasn't supposed to know he was in a policeman's house. He was told it was a "big dealer". Explaining that he wanted to get many Kilos, 20 or 30 at least, and he would need help packing it in the doors and under the seats Paco was told "oh yes senor we can do all of that".

A huge sack of pot was dragged out and Paco pretended to haggle over the price. Finally settling on maybe 25 kilos @ 30 dollars a kilo. ($750.00 US about twice the normal price) "All right then", it was all agreed. Paco would return with the hustler at 8:00 P.M. the next night. He would bring "his partner with the money" and they would all help him pack the car for the "smuggling run" up north.

"Just one thing", (solo una cosa) Paco said. "I need a sample for my partner with the money so he knows it's for real". His eyes shining with excitement at not only getting Paco's money for the pot but the reward he would get when he routinely informed to US Customs, the Official folded a piece of newspaper, put a few large handfuls from the bushel sack inside, and gave it to Paco. "Es muy bueno" he assured Paco. With many mutual assurances of exactly when and where they should meet the next evening Paco was guided back to the neighborhood near his Hotel. Entering their room he called out "honey, I got something to smoke".

They left town early the next morning.

Retrieving the car from the shop they left Guadalajara and drove to where a tourist map indicated there was a Major Highway connecting Guadalajara and Puerto Vallarta in what appeared to be a straight line Due West. The road was right there on a brochure Paco had picked up at the Hotel and they were mystified when nobody seemed to be able to tell them where it was. Finally driving to where they figured it should be they started due west along a paved road that quickly turned into a dirt track.

Instead of retracing their steps and heading north to Tepic and then south to go around the forbidding Sierra Madres mountain range Paco was convinced that the wide green line on the tourist map was the "new Highway" to PV. After all, the brochure said so. Finally the road ceased to be a road and about the place it turned into a rutted trail they had come to a check point manned by half a dozen wide brimmed mustachioed "Federal Pistoleros". Unlike the banditos or even regular Federalies these guys were clean, alert, and had well worn expensive low slung strapped down real McCoy six shooters. They were very jovial and polite however and Paco noticed that some had bullet furrows on their cheeks and scalps. "Where are you going?" they asked. Maya said "Marscota", naming the only large town on the map halfway between the two points.

"You can't get through the road doesn't exist" they were told. "There must be some road," they said. "The government has not built the new road yet, senor. Trust me you cannot get through." "We are going to try anyway," said Paco who was a little reluctant to go back to Guadalajara. "But there is no police in those mountains", said the handsome young gunslinger with sincere concern. "We are the last government police you will see, and when we go in there we always travel together. It is wild in there and not safe."

Reasoning that there had to be some sort of road to Marscota and determined to move on and cover some ground before dark, Paco and Maya went ahead anyway. Navigating west by the setting sun and leaving the posse (for that's what it was) scratching their heads and making the sign of the cross. "Fools rush in where Angels fear to tread".

They drove on the dusty track which after a while got a little better' "see" they said. "What do these guys know".

They rolled along and after nightfall camped by the side of the "road". They hadn't seen a soul.

The next morning they continued and came to a little village. The people seemed amazed to see them and waved. "This is going to be all right" they thought. They continued on what they thought was west but couldn't keep track because the road twisted in all directions as the terrain became steeper and they climbed and climbed reaching higher and higher elevations. There were no guardrails and the road was one lane wide deeply rutted and potholed. Dipping into a pothole they lost the muffler. It was still there but no longer attached. Every once in a while it would bash another rock. "I'll have to get that fixed," thought Paco. They sounded pretty loud but got used to it.

On the downside of a mountain at about 10,000 feet elevation on a sharp curve the steering wheel broke loose. One moment it was connected to the wheels and the next moment it wasn't. Because they were moving slowly (the road had become rugged and very rocky) the brakes immediately stopped the car inches from the edge of a 5 thousand-foot drop. Paco was a little rattled, first of all the drop off to the valley below was just inches from the front wheel and if the steering was gone that far into the bush then there would be no hope of salvaging their possessions. Maya suggested that the locals would use the rotting olds for a chicken coop and they both started laughing. It was a great moment. Stuck on the edge of a high precipice with broken steering in the completely inappropriate vehicle for the terrain they were overcome by the staggering beauty of the mountain valleys stretching away thousands of feet beneath them.

While living in Spain they had ridden on a long slow 3rd class train which wound through the mountains of Andalucia. They had watched as an elderly couple had made lunch together. Each did their part in the process, peeling the fruit and cutting the cheese, breaking the bread in such a quiet natural way that it was obvious that they had been together for a lifetime. Paco and Maya both were moved "Let's be like that" they both said.

Maya made lunch, and Paco opened the hood. Right in plain sight and easily accessible was a knuckle joint that had lost the pin holding it together. They ate lunch sitting on the hood of the car with their backs against the windshield and marveled at the pristine beauty stretched out below them. Then Paco made a new pin for the knuckle joint out of a heavy metal coat hanger that he found in the trunk and they continued.

The roads were a little better in the low lands. The problem is that the only lowlands were the valley floors that went for a few miles before the road headed for the sky again and always got worse as it went higher up.

They came to a village with a little store that sold Chiclets and Pepsi. Most of the few other vehicles they had seen were cattle trucks, which must have come up the river beds because the high roads were barely wide enough for the Olds. They had seen riders on horseback, some wagons, some cattle, and an occasional Jeep. The villagers laughed with delight at the old green car, and the wild-eyed (the police chiefs pot was great) "American Gypsies" who careened through their villages into the unknown. "Marscota?" Paco and Maya would yell as they passed and with wide grins the smiling Indio's would point the way. "This isn't so bad" thought Paco, "we'll be in Marscota by tonight."

For the next three days they struggled with the incredible terrain. They needed information so Maya asked those who spoke Spanish about how far it was to Marscota and what were the road conditions. The answers were vague on distance but they were told a few times that "you can get to Marscota, but you can't get from there to Puerto Vallarta. You have to cross a deep wide river that is much too high for your car." Only in the dry season could it possibly be done.

They were able to "top off" their gas at a ranch that had a tractor.

The switchbacks and climbing and descending continued. They replenished their food with fresh fruit and Fanta. They got water from small waterfalls that cascaded down the mountainsides. They had a store of dried fruit and nuts they had brought from the states. That and tortillas with beans or canned sardines were available at tiny shacks for the vaqueros on horseback who rode through.

Sometimes they would climb way up a mountain on a narrow dangerous track with no shoulder and would find the road just stopped with a 20 or 30 foot gap. They later found out that the Airline which flew from Guadalajara to PV had sent vaqueros out on horseback with dynamite to blow the road up on the high pass's so the tourist trade would remain air accessible only. It was these men that the Posse they had passed had been chasing. It was the Airlines and Movie Stars (who liked their privacy) lobby group that was responsible for the road not being built that was on Paco's brochure map.

None of that helped Paco and Maya who, had they known, would have gone north through Tepic.

Where the road was blown away they would have to back miles down the mountain, leave the roadway and find a way around the mountain to rejoin what they hoped would be the road. They would wait for the occasional cattle truck and then follow it. They followed one big cattle truck through a forest and down a riverbed. Paco marveled that the Olds made it back to the road No one would stop and the Indians they met on horseback didn't appear to speak any Spanish. They had never seen a Gringo before and were utterly amazed.

Their oil pan was punctured by a rock. They had half a case in the trunk (the Olds burned oil) so they jacked the car up onto rocks, removed the pan, reshaped it with a rock, fixed the hole with the solder and refilled it.

They had three flat tires, the first was no big deal. They put on the spare. The second made things difficult and really slowed them down. With the nose of the Olds tilted left they ground on riding on the rim. Paco believed that the further they went the less distance they would have to walk so they moved on at about 5 miles an hour making an eerie grinding noise in addition to the growling (now mufferless) engine. The rim grinding into the rutted road did have one advantage, it held them locked to the rut and lessened the danger of going off those jaw-dropping cliffs that were often inches from their front or rear wheels

After 5 days torturous negotiation of the barrancos and barrancas of the Sierra Madres Late in the evening, riding on two tires and two rims, ("one in the back for traction and one in the front for steering" Paco said), they arrived at the inaccessible 10,000 foot high mountain city of Marscota. It was small but it was formidable. There were big old 17th century buildings with classical Spanish balconies that looked out over the surrounding valleys marching off below. The walls of the courtyards were very high and looked about three feet thick. They stopped in the center by a fountain and marveled at what seemed like "civilization". It looked like something out of a time capsule.

They were approached be a colorful gentleman wearing a hat that must have been three feet across at the brim. He carried what was "fashion de jour" for the gentry, a pearl handled 45. This guy was pleased and amazed to see them. Paco realized they had not seen another passenger car in the entire five days. The Jefe said he was an important man and that they were invited to stay at his house and rest and refresh themselves. After all he said, they were the first tourists to ever come there and it was his duty to welcome them. Paco was reluctant. He was used to guys trying to hit on Maya and didn't want any trouble. He touched his forefinger to his right cheek in the sign for "watch out"

The guy was insistent and warned that they would not be safe if they camped out in the old cobblestone streets. Maya listened to the guy talk and thought he sounded legit, so she made a small motion with her right hand palm down as though she was sliding her hand under something. It meant "its ok". So they drove the olds through the high gates of a big corner house into a courtyard and were welcomed by the family.

Maya chattered in Spanish and soon they had hot food. Chicken and rice with raisins. Green salad with tomatoes and avocado's. They were shown to an alcove/room off the courtyard near their car and slept like logs under the protection of the Jefe.

In the morning they set out again. Two flat tires at five miles an hour meant that ten hours later they had covered maybe fifty miles. Now the terrain took them down and down with switchbacks, potholes and ruts. Except for the cobblestones in Marscota it was their 6th day without seeing a paved road.

At least they had a road to follow and they were lower down. Maybe they would make it.

Paco began driving a little faster. In the dark they were moving downhill. The road twisted left then right then wasn't there at all. All of a sudden they were in a small fast moving river.

As they had driven off a steep bank into the river that had washed out the road, Paco had gunned the engine trying to leap the gap. They were three quarters of the way across but they were stuck and stuck good. The car had landed like a ton of bricks. The banks were steep and by gunning the engine Paco had almost made it. The hood was far enough out of the water on the opposite bank so that the engine still ran. Paco tried to move the car but there was no traction from the rear wheels. Well, one wheel and a rim. He turned off the engine.

The water was up to the windows. The noise of the river rushing past was quite loud. It was pitch dark.

Maya turned to him. "Paco man" she said, "I have to tell you that at this moment I am more scared then I have ever been in my entire life. I am completely freaked. If you can work your magic and please, please, please, get me out of this river I will love you for the rest of your life. No matter what, forever".

She was shivering. A sense of profound compassion overwhelmed Paco. He saw that Maya was staring strangely and biting her lip. He dove out the window. The water was cold but woke him up.

Diving and feeling underneath the back of the car Paco could feel that the wheels were not making contact with anything. In order to get out he would need both tires on the rear axle and something to drive on. Working under water in the dark Paco first jacked up the side with the tire and gathering large flat stones he built a flat track for the tire to rest on and drive out on. He repeated the process on the other side and taking the front tire off and exchanging it for the rear rim he mounted the two good tires on the rear with a series of rocks piled up to ride on.

He got back in and held his breath when he tried the engine. What a car, it started with the muffler pipe bubbling underwater. He dropped it into drive and floored it. It blasted out of the river like a shot out of a cannon. It was quite remarkable.

Paco paused to switch one of the two back tires to the tireless front, and Maya said "thank you". Her eyes were shining.

They continued to grind their way down. They calculated that given speed and distance they should be close to a village maybe ten miles above "the big river".

They nearly made it.

This time the road dipped sharply and dumped them into a wider river. Not "the big river" (Rio Americus) but big enough. Paco gunned the engine but they were stuck right smack dab in the middle of the crossing point. They were up to their hubs on all four wheels in the riverbed. The engine died. That was it.

Maya said in a calm voice "it's alright, I'm ok now. It was the last river that scared me. You really came through for me. You don't have to do that again. I want you to know that what ever happens now I'm ok. What ever happens it will be all right". Maya's instincts had been quite correct in regard to the first river. Years later Paco came back in the daylight, and saw the 2000 foot drop that had been only a few feet down stream from where we had been stuck.

Now in the wide moonlit river it was obvious that they were in no immediate danger. The water wasn't moving that fast and wasn't that deep, maybe the tops of the wheels. There was no sense of urgency and the moon had come out from the clouds. The stars twinkled. They rolled a joint of the police chief's pot. They sat and considered a plan to move their possessions to the opposite bank and go for help in the morning. The village couldn't be that much further. In fact it was less then a mile. Before they found that out they were sitting in the dead car in the middle of the river smoking a joint and laughing at their predicament when they saw lights headed toward them fast. "A truck" said one. "Maybe they can help pull us out", said the other.

It was a truck alright. It was three armed rustlers and a stolen bull in a four-wheel drive farm truck. They were making their getaway from somewhere further towards the coast, and were in a big hurry. A posse was sure to be in hot pursuit. Their lives depended on their escape towards Marscota. Paco and Maya had the shallow crossing blocked like a cork. No way around and no way through.

They tried backing down the bank and after hooking a rope to the Olds they pulled. The Olds didn't budge. The rope broke. Throughout all of this the bull bellowed and roared. With the sound bouncing off the river canyon walls it was eerie and unbelievably loud. The rustlers were sweating and frantic. They huddled for a minute and then leaving one of their gang to guard Paco and Maya with a drawn 45. They disappeared with the truck and the bellowing bull towards the village.

 Maya learned later that they had woken up the entire village and at gunpoint had commandeered two other four-wheel drive cattle trucks. Returning with the other trucks the three trucks had spread out in a fan shape on the far bank and in the now bright moonlight they all attached ropes and pulled together. The olds came out of the river.

The moment it was clear of the ford the rustlers jumped in their truck and with the bull still bellowing at the top of his lungs they sped across and up thc other bank towards the hills. One of the local farm trucks towed the olds to the village.

Paco and Maya spent what was left of the night sleeping in a hammock in the only little store in the village. They awoke and had a wash and some food. Then for 15 or 20 dollars Paco arranged to have the Olds taken to Puerto Vallarta on the back of a large cattle truck. Big boards were produced for a ramp and the whole town turned out to push the dripping Olds up onto the truck bed. Riding in the cab of the truck for the last 30 miles into PV, they crossed the big river they had been told about. It was very wide and deep in the middle. The high axeled cattle truck pitched and rocked but made it easily.

The truck dumped them (and the Olds) off on "the Malecon" in the heart of beautiful downtown Puerto Vallarta. It was a beautiful day and they had arrived. It was the first and only time that anyone had ever brought a 2-wheel drive vehicle from Guadalajara to Puerto Vallarta by way of Marscota. They made arrangements for some used tires and a battery charge, and went looking for a house to rent.

That evening as they were eating their dinner after they watched the sunset on the beach they had to giggle. They still had 2 ounces of the police chief's pot.

PUERTO VALLARTA

January 1965

PV (as it was called) was a small fishing town with two cobblestoned streets running parallel to the beach and cobblestoned side streets connecting the two. The hotels were along the "Malecon" facing the beach and began from the large plaza with the church and ran to the small plaza with the market about half a mile away. The old town was across the river to the south and the unpaved roads were dusty and charming. The old town had its own beach called "Los Muertos" (The beach of the dead men). Aptly named because it was at the time infested with venomous sea snakes, which were small and nonaggressive but were attracted to the lights along the beach. The tourist office told everyone they were harmless and during their time there no one was bitten that they heard of although they saw hundreds of them. There were other snakes too but that comes later.

There were few cars because the only road in was to the north and was nearly impassable. Lack of bridges, potholes, washed out roads, made the one lane road impossible except in 4 wheel drive vehicles and was impassable altogether during parts of the rainy season in the summer. Also there were Bandits.

Their first day down at the beach hey encountered an interesting "ex-pat" named Jungle Jim who was married to a Mexican Woman. She was an established beautiful cultured, educated Mexican woman who had a house and walled garden in the Old Town. Jim had what was at the time the only beach house down at the south end of "Los Muertos" It was a great little house. Perched on the rocks above the crashing surf, Jim had built and improved it over time. He had been there for 50 years and was a fixture. They became friends with Jim and his wife Josefa. Jim told them stories of local lore, which explained many things.

One of the first local stories that they heard from Jim was how, some year's back, there had been one particular bandit who had regularly closed the road from the nofth. He was well known for going through lady tourist's luggage and examining their underwear. He was a jovial colorful character who looked a lot like the old pictures of Pancho Villa complete with 3-foot sombrero, crossed ammo belts, and rifle. In fact, Pancho had ridden with Villa. His view was that sovereignty over the road was his just reward for his part in the liberation of Mexico. His name was Pancho Lepe. He had a great sense of humor, a terrific appreciation of the ladies, and a slightly larcenous nature. He was a great man. His children became some of the greatest artists in all of Mexico. President Luis Echeverria named his son, Manuel Lepe, "National Painter of Mexico". Collectors from every country bought his paintings.

Mexicans are great pragmatists. Some years before Paco and Maya's arrival the tourist board had gone out on the road and approached Pancho. "Pancho, how can we ever develop a tourist industry if you rob all the tourists, and some of the woman are complaining really loud. Pancho you shouldn't ask to see their breasts some of them may be Catholic". "Pancho",

the emissary continued, "we will give you an entire square block in the old town if you will come in out of the hills. Just think, Pancho, you can rent little casitas to all the tourists girls and look over the wall into their courtyards. Also we will not have to bring an army to hunt you down and kill you."
Pancho was doubtful that any army could find him in those hills below Marscota but was secretly delighted and accepted. Thus he became the proprietor of an entire block in the old town with a dozen little 2-room apartments with small courtyards that faced the center of the block. The courtyards had 7-foot high walls with glass on top, but that didn't stop Pancho from peeking over. The place was popular with many of the beautiful people who sunbathed nude including a famous Swedish actress and John D. Barryless the famous actor. It was central and cheap and for the ladies Pancho would make little taco treats. It was actually totally charming.

The lack of accessibility made PV an ideal watering hole for the rich and famous. John D. lived on the low end of the economic scale but had one of the few cars. A Chrysler Station Wagon with AC and a great sound system. Steve

McQueen lived where the river met the sea and had the toughest dog in town. (A weimeraner). Brando was building a mansion above "Playa Conchas Chinas" (beach of the chinese shells). Liz Taylor was still around. Francis Ford Coppola was building his own village a few miles down the coast. It was a great scene. It was primitive but for all intents and purposes it was Paradise. Jet set people who spent their summers on Ibiza spent their winters in PV. There were great restaurants, cheap accommodations, great food, and horses. It was a perfect environment to rest from their travels and heal.

They found a house several blocks back from the beach in the old town. One of a group of three it had one bedroom a small living area and a large bath. The kitchen was large and under a porch and had a nice high walled garden with a substantial gate. It was $65.00 per month and they paid 4 months in advance.

They explored the town and found places to buy the ingredients for their diet. Shrimp from a freezer, which meant paella, ground beef from another small freezer, which meant cheeseburgers. Rice and other staples like cereal honey and milk. Fresh fruit was nearly free. They found out that they could rent horses for 40 cents an hour.

They swam in the day, rode horses in the morning first along the beach and then to market. The man that owned the string of horses kept two mounts just for them and fed them extra oats. Paco rode a palomino and Maya road a black mare. The vaquero would send his son to drop them off and pick them up at their house. They took siestas in the afternoon and often went out to dinner at night. They hung out with their neighbors. One was a couple from New Jersey who had been there several months, and the other neighbors were two guys from Hollywood. Harry and Larry they were trying to be cool but weren't quite making it. They trotted out some pot but compared to the pot that Paco and Maya had brought with them it was "basura" (garbage). They put candles around the garden path and enjoyed the ripe mangoes that fell from the old tree that provided shade in their garden..

When Paco first went to the beach he wore his hat and dark glasses, and long pants. Eventually he shed his clothes and his reticent attitude. Later he would ride down to the beach on horseback wearing shorts and sandals. Most of the resident guys went body surfing so Paco learned how and surfed every day. What with the galloping horseback rides, the good food, the sun and the outdoor exercise they both quickly became brown and healthy. Maya turned dark and her hair became bleached by the sun. She looked terrific and started to make her own clothes collaborating with Josefa who had a factory system set up with local labor to copy NY styles. For Maya the challenge was how to make local materials into cool clothes. She bought cloth in the local stores and made a whole line of "granny gowns" that were soon copied all over town by the young girls. Easy to make from different local fabrics they became quite popular.

Paco saw many opportunities for export using the low cost labor. Jungle Jim cautioned him "remember the story of the baskets". " What's that"? Said Paco. So Jim told him.

It was a popular local story and Jim swore it was true. It seems that a tourist from NY had come down on a plane and spent a week at one of the hotels on the Malecon. While out on a guided horseback ride in the jungle behind the town he had encountered an old man sitting by the side of the trail selling baskets. There were several on a blanket and the tourist bought one for 12 pesos (one dollar). It was a nice basket. Back in the hotel room the man from NY stared at the basket. Only one dollar, he mused, why my friend in the candy business would pay 5 or 6 dollars for a basket like that. Heck my friend in the flower business might pay 7. He started to get excited as he thought of all the possibilities and profit to be made from such great baskets at $1.00@. He couldn't sleep. He caught the first plane back to NY in the morning. 1st he went to his friend the candy maker and based on the sample got an order for 10,000 at $5.00 @. Next he went to his friend the flower wholesaler and got an order for 8 thousand more at 6.00 @. He was pumped. Lets see he thought $98,000.00 gross minus $18,000.00 for the baskets leaves $80,000.00 profit for me. He was so excited he had to pee. He caught the first plane back to Mexico in the morning.

Deciding that with so much at stake he shouldn't alarm the old man he hired a guide and horses and found the old man by the roadside. Some shaft of reality must have penetrated so he asked the Old Man "errrr how long would it take to make say, he wanted to say 5 thousand but decided to go slow at first". "How about 500 baskets" he finally said. "Ohhh, senor, that is many baskets you will have to come back in three days for me to tell you. Would the senor also want to know the price?" Thinking that the old man meant a quantity discount the entrepreneur from NY said "sure". He fretted for three days by the pool at the hotel and then returned. "Well" he said "how long and how much". "Well senor the old man said we can have them for you in a few weeks". "That's great" thought the entrepreneur, "it's a good start". "OK" he said "how much?" "Ohhh senor they will be $7.00.00@". "How can that be" the man shrieked "it was a dollar for one 5 days ago". "Si senor that is true but I cannot make all those baskets so the whole family will have to help. My daughters can no longer go to work for the gringos, the cane will have to be cut and then brought in by burros, Then it must be dried and turned. The whole village is willing to help but they will all have to give up their other occupations. They too must live senor. The best price we can do is $7.00@." As the old man went on and on detailing how they had arrived at the price the entrepreneur from NYC realized that his dream of instant wealth was shattered. Like many before him.

Paco too had had bad experiences trying to accelerate production in Mexico. Haste meant waste, and cheap goods tended to have bad wood that couldn't survive the climate change. For example the Mexicans handmade some great guitars but the cheap ones didn't last more than a couple months up north.

Through surfing Paco met another permanent resident, a young man who was called "The Wheel". This was an interesting person for a few reasons. 1st was his amazing command of Spanish. He not only spoke fluent Spanish with several regional accents but he had mastered most of the various Indian dialects as well. He would amaze Maya with his obscure idioms and literacy in the Spanish culture. 2nd was his black passport. It turned out that "The Wheel" was the son of a former US Ambassador to France. That rated him a black passport as a family member of a diplomat. For the "Wheel" it meant guaranteed kid gloves handling.

3rd "The Wheel was a master smuggler who was active in bringing in what was for that time large amounts of pot into the us and creating a distribution network in several cities. The demand for pot was increasing rapidly as the underground and antiwar movement began to get up a head of steam. "The Wheel" was a major supplier to the US at the time. It took all of the Wheels language skills to work with farmers high in the mountains who each grew perhaps 12 or 15 Kilos tops. After all they, like the old man by the roadside with the hats, only supplied a small local market. "The Wheel" traveled into all the back hill areas from Sinaloa through Michoacan, and on south armed and accompanied by an armed bodyguard to contract for these small crops. Picking them up at the end of the growing season they would assemble them for shipment north.

Various people had their small ways. One guy sailed north each year in a small catamaran. The hulls would be packed with pot. To the US coast guard he just looked like a guy out for a day sale and never bothered him. He did it once a year and lived off the profits.

"The Wheel" was thinking big however. He was working on the first 1000 pound smuggle in history. It would break all records. Just putting it together required almost a years work.

"The wheel" was very intelligent and educated and was fun to hang around with. A little reserved and serious he was a force to be reckoned with. He had a fabulous horse named "Talisman" that was half Arab and could do 27 tricks. This guy was no slouch.

Another Major player on the scene was a Guru named Tom Newman. "The Wheel" was Tom's protégé. It was Tom Newman who had been the Wheels tutor in tradecraft and working within the Mexican system. Tom had been in Mexico for 50 years at least and really knew how to get by.

He would create an illusion in the officials eyes with meaningless paperwork and could always read the signs of a scene. He had never been caught or charged with anything. He was an original Psychedelic Guru. He knew where the Mushrooms grew of fabled lore. He knew when they grew and which ones were which. He knew the side effects of each of the 8 sub-varieties of the psilocybin mushroom. He knew how to manipulate the extrasensory perception aspect of these rare funguses. He was quite the warlock. Tom had taught "the Wheel" several of his trade secrets, which included how to obtain LSD and Mescaline from French Chemical Supply Houses. These supply houses had no problem shipping to Dr. Newman's "research Laboratory" in Mexico. With access to chemically pure Psychedelics Tom and The Wheel had a monopoly on the LSD culture of PV. The rich and famous were curious and so were the Movie Stars. Tom did a brisk trade and often had the use of a mansion as his headquarters.

There was one other person who made up their immediate circle. It was J D. Barryless the famous actor. Barryless was a blast. Constantly posing in one of the swashbuckling scenes from his father's movies he was brilliant and entertaining. At the time he was a well-known western actor. Maya and JD's Swedish movie star girlfriend hit it off and got along great. After all they were both drop dead gorgeous.

JD was more fun than puppies to go out riding with. Barryless could do all the tricks that everyone has seen in the movies. Mounting with a leap over the rear. Riding under the neck, ducking off the side and back up. Turning around in the saddle. He could dismount at a full gallop bounce his heels on the ground and bounce back up into the saddle. He had great balance and was a natural gymnast. They often all went thundering down the coast together towards Playa Conchas Chinas and became friends.

Not everyone supported this concept of happy experimenters living in relative fabulous luxury and contentment in paradise.

These people were having fun and it was the sworn duty of special agent Dweeb the number two Agent of the Federal Narcotics Bureau. He was head of the New York Office and was second in rank only to Harry Anslinger. He had been sent down their to investigate based on a complaint from the Burned Detective Agency. In Dweeb's mind he represented the power, the might and the majesty that was the US of A. No body was going to have fun living in paradise and taking drugs if he had anything to say about it.

He was overcome by his own outrage. One night J.D Barryless, Tom Newman, Paco and Maya, the Swedish star, and a few others were having dinner at a long table at a nice restaurant. Special Agent Dweeb just lost it, he couldn't control himself. He stood near the table and threw a fit. The sight of these happy beautiful people just blew his cork. He must have an unhappy life, thought Paco as he watched the froth come from the mans mouth. Poor agent Dweeb. He had no jurisdictional authority and these people were flaunting the laws (of the US). They were obviously having a total blast doing it too. When he was finished they all raised their glasses and toasted his performance. It just made him more pissed and he stormed off. That was interesting thought Paco. Wonder what's next.

One day to Paco's amazement John Wayne was standing in the Plaza. Paco had gotten the Olds running for a few days and drove around the plaza twice. He was very impressed. It turned out the "the Duke" was there to see Barryless. As he heard it later The Duke came to Pancho Lepe's and tried to talk John into coming back to the States with him on his yacht which was moored in the bay. "Well go fishing" said the Duke. Johns Mother was worried about John and had sent the Duke to try to convince him to return. John said "no, no, no". If you saw the Swedish star you wouldn't blame him John Wayne sailed off into the Sunset without Barryless. He had good reason to worry however.

Something happened which would bring Paco and Barryless closer together as friends.

One evening a few days after the Duke had left Paco stopped by the Wheels house to make a payment on the horse Talisman. Paco had made a deal to buy the Arabian from the Wheel as a gift for Maya. The house was down by the beach

and the noise of the surf made his hello go unheard so he
entered.

He walked through the living room and into the bedroom.
John was laid out on the bed and the Wheel was reading to
him. It sounded like an instruction manual. "What's up
guys?" said Paco "shhh" said the Wheel "this isn't a good
time," JD is tripping. "Wow" said Paco "on how much
what?" "5 grams of Mescaline" came Barryless's voice from
the bed , a little disembodied. For some reason the Wheel left
the room and Paco said to JD "that's much to much. And you
shouldn't be letting people read stuff into your brain in that
condition. But 5 grams is way too much." Paco was very
concerned. One gram was a full blown intense experience.
Five grams was way off the charts. Paco was far more
comfortable with a fifth of a gram on the rare occasion when
he took psychedelics. There were ethics involved here it was
Paco's obligation to help JD through it and ease him down
without trauma. "Hey JD", Paco said "wanna cheeseburger?.
How about a cheeseburger made be Maya and some really
good smoke." JD was interested (he liked Maya). Like a far-

gone drunk his head lifted and he slurred "tha shounds like a good idea les go." So Paco helped him up and towards the door. The Wheel came back and was very upset. "Where are you going?" "Going with Paco, getta cheeseburger and a pipe." JD was like Frank Sinatra playing the drunken Maggio in From Here to Eternity. The Wheel was really agitated. Whatever he had in mind for JD it was canceled now. Paco thought that his friend was being brainwashed and just wanted to get him out of there. There was no arguing with JD when he had made his mind up. After all he was a star. So over the Wheels vigorous objections they left and went to Paco's house. Maya made cheeseburgers, and they smoked and played music in the candlelit garden until dawn when the mescaline finally started to wear off and JD was able to go back to Pancho Lepe's and get some sleep.

One of the reasons JD Barryless had been so willing to go with Paco was because Paco had something to put in the pipe the was better than anything else around even for the rich and famous. He had hash. The local pot wasn't that strong. The beach boys sold bags to the tourists but they all got it from an old man who came in from the hills with a donkey and an occasional Kilo.

One night Paco and Maya had been sitting around the garden with Harry and Larry telling stories of Tangier when the thought occurred to both of them at the same time. Maybe it isn't Cannabis Indicta but maybe it would be possible to make Hash out of Cannabis Sativa. Paco wondered if it would work. He wondered what the yield would be and started to calculate Kilo price vs. finished hash price. Only one way to find out. He bribed a beach boy to find the old man who was the grower and made contact. He bought a kilo and some screens etc and processed it. It yielded 50 grams of very credible hash for a 20-dollar investment. They gave it away and traded a few grams for various things like diving fins and snorkel masks. It was an instant sensation. The problem was that he only had a little. He bought three more Kilos and turned out 150 grams (less than 6 ounces) it disappeared in a couple weeks. It was very very popular. 1st of all most people had never even seen it, only heard of it. 2nd it was very good. It really got you high. It certainly made them popular. It also attracted more heat. Agent Dweeb had apparently returned to his duties as number two narc under Anslinger in charge of the NYC office. There the opportunities to extort bribe and steal would keep him busy and out of the hair of the happy little group down in PV. Others were on their way however.

JD expressed his appreciation to Paco for "his rescue" by tearing the terrific sound system out of his car and giving it to him. JD was finally leaving and wanted Paco to have it and the tapes that went with it. Paco was overwhelmed and as JD left he gave JD one of his best new pieces of hash. It was finger shaped and very dark brown. JD said "When you leave come to Hollywood where you will be Hashmaker to the stars"

"Sounds like a plan", thought Paco.

On his way back to the States JD 1st drove to Tepic and then down to Guadalajara to visit his "Batman" who was serving time on some drug charge at the Guadalajara prison. After visiting JD was leaving when he was stopped and searched by an alert Police Official who had been told that he was there.

This same Official was still smarting from some smart aleck getting a three ounce free sample and not returning to be busted a few months before and was eager to bust the famous star to regain his status. They found the piece of hash. The Jefe was delighted. Ohhhh boy, we got you now Barryless, your rich mama gonna have to pay big pesos to get you back again now. You gonna be in a cell with your fren." The Jefe spoke to his assistant Manuel, "here" he said "rush this opium down to the lab and get proof that it's opium so we can take Senor Barryless to the alcalde for arraignment". In an hour or so while JD sweated on a wooden bench Manuel came rushing back. "Jefe, Jefe", he said. "Is not opio". "Not opio" said the Jefe. "What is it"? "We don't know Jefe all we know is that we tested it for opio and it wasn't". Scratching their heads they let J.D. Barryless go.

About that time with their heightened status and relative stability they were offered the beach house of Jungle Jim's for a few weeks. It was a great interlude, on the rocks above the crashing surf they enjoyed the staggering views of the sunsets and the dolphins jumping in the shafts of moonlight on the water. The formations of seabirds that flew past their balcony and the waving palm trees added to the feeling of "Paradise".

Paco went skin diving everyday and learned the location of all the underwater grottos near by. One day he went out and on the rocks at the end of the beach pretending to be fishing was "Dr.Oswald Lesummer". Paco had met Oswald at one of his Hootenannies in Boston and knew Oswald was some kind of cop. Exactly what flavor Paco wasn't sure. What a small world said Paco, "Oswald what are you doing here"? Oswald proclaimed that "he was there on a "Fact Finding Mission" for the "New York State Narcotics Commission". "Wow that's a mouth full" Paco said. "exactly what kind of facts were they trying to find?"

"This town has a reputation for LSD and Psychedelics" said Oswald. Oswald was so out of the loop that Paco regarded him much like one would a foolish child. One thing was for sure Oswald had no actual authority in Mexico and was thus not to be feared. Paco wondered what role Maya's father had in instigating this "Fact Finding Mission".

Oswald told him he was with an Official from some Federal Agency in Chicago that had jurisdiction over the Midwest and they both were staying in one of the humungous mansions above the Beach House where Paco and Mays were staying.

Paco was amused and not intimidated. After all he had broken no US Laws, recently anyway. Toying with Oswald Paco watched him fish for a moment or two and said "you know you are doing it all wrong. Your not even believable as a fisherman how can you find out any facts." "Wadaya mean" said the somewhat rotund and sweating Oswald (who had really been faking fishing). "Cast your line over by that rock said Pablo." Pablo was intimate with the underwater terrain and knew the rock was the tip on a car-size underwater grotto wherein lived a large fat Bonita about 2 feet long. Oswald did. Instantly the fish struck with a boil of water. Oswald nearly dropped his pole. He grabbed it back and pulled trying to get hold of the reel to crank it in. He was incredibly excited. Paco thought that he must have never caught a fish before. It was about a 6-pound fish and put up the fight of its life. Finally after a few minutes of intense thrashing it came to an end.

Leaping out of the water the fish caught the line on the sharp edge of the rocky grotto and broke free. Paco was glad for the fish. Oswald was panting and gasping. He was radiant. "That's the most exciting thing that ever happened to me", he said. "How did you do that. How did you know it was there?" he asked, peering intently, looking for all the world like a plump nearsighted happy child.

"It's the LSD" said Paco, "it makes you able to see through rocks and water. Would you like to try some"?

Oswald was shocked. He had begun his day planning to encounter and reconnoiter. He never expected this level of success. He found himself completely outmaneuvered. "Tell you what", said Paco "we will come to your house tonight about 8. You can introduce your friend and we will bring a couple girls for you and your friend". Since it was Oswald's plan to be overtly social Paco was determined to outdo him. After all they knew the town really well by then.

 At 8 PM Paco and Maya showed up. They brought along two ladies they knew who were there for the season from the Costa del Sol in Spain. One of the ladies had a couple caps of acid and after introduction offered both men a "tab". The guy from Chicago seemed like quite a decent sort Paco thought. Younger than Oswald he seemed a little idealistic and a little unsure of the propriety of his mission. How do you know its bad if you haven't taken it? Paco asked.

Paco was very curious to see if Oswald would take Acid and watched him carefully. The girls were quite attractive and the one with the tabs started hanging out with the representative from Chicago. Paco was convinced that Oswald had palmed his and pretended to take it. As time went on it became obvious that Oswald wasn't "on board". As time passed it became obvious that the guy from Chicago had taken his.

"Let's have some music," the Chicago guy said. One of the girls disappeared for a few minutes in the Jeep that came with all rental mansions and was back in half an hour followed a few minutes later by a 10 piece Mariachi Band. They played all night for ten pesos a song.

Hours passed and the Chicago guy now in the most magnanimous of moods handed out a bottle of booze to each member of the band. The band members looked at each other and never stopped playing the entire night except to swig a little. Paco and Maya showered and cleaned up in the big tile bathroom that had a view of the sea. They chatted and smoked with the other one of the girls from Spain whom Oswald had showed no interest in. "That loser" thought Paco, "he's so hot to get back to the US with his palmed evidence of wrongdoing he's passing up the chance for some world class nookie. Should have given him a vitamin pill". They sat on the stone abutment that jutted out from the hillside and looked at the stars. At some point while Oswald sat on the sofa and pretended to act a little drunk the gentleman from Chicago disappeared into one to the bedrooms with the pretty girl from the Costa del Sol.

Around 3 in the morning they decided to walk down the path to the beach and go home. Before they left they stopped back into the house to say goodnight. Oswald was sitting bolt upright on the couch watching through half closed slits of eyes pretending to weave and be woosey. The 10 Piece Mariachi band were performing Malaguenas Por Sala Rosa for the 25th time. The number three Federal Narcotics Agent in the United States, head of the Chicago Field Office, with jurisdiction over the entire Midwest, was standing on top of the railing of the balcony. With the sea crashing a couple hundred feet directly behind him. He was stark naked, and was conducting the inebriated but straight-faced mariachi band with a long stem rose. As they walked down the path back to their beach house they looked back and saw the naked conductor still waving his rose baton.

They heard later that the guy from Chicago left on the 1st flight out in the early morning. It seemed that he had some sort of insight and couldn't wait to share it with his family.

Oswald left later in the day. He knew that Paco knew that he was a fraud and couldn't face him.

A couple days later Paco and Maya went back to their own house several blocks back from the beach.

PUERTO VALLARTA SUMMER 1965

Paco and Maya moved to the other end of town. It wasn't for any special reason, it just worked out that way. Harry and Larry had left to go back to the states taking all of Paco's product to date with them. That left Paco and Maya solvent with a few hundred dollars but their instincts told them it was time to move. They heard of a house for rent high on a hill at the other end of PV, and decided a change of neighborhood would be interesting. It was a nice large house with a garden and a guesthouse and the rainy season was fast approaching. They had been pretty flagrant where they were for quite a few months. Part of the Hash making process involved making the "pieces" out of the extracted resin. The Cannabis Sativa extract had different adhesion properties then its Cannabis Indicta cousin. The "hot knife" method didn't work very well. So Paco experimented with heating up a tortilla press on the stove, putting the resin in a cloth bag, jacking the Olds up in the air and then dropping the front end on top of the red hot

press containing the bag from a height of three or four feet.
(Don't try this at home) It worked all right but not that great.
It was labor intensive, made a lot of noise and the Mexican
neighbor's thought he was nuts.

Paco had gotten hold of a microscope somewhere and was
engaged in intensive "research" on how to raise the quality of
the yield of resin from the Cannabis Sativa plant. Like some
tropical scientist he bent over his microscope and studied
slides he made from the extracted resin. To bind it together
he finally resorted to an ancient method from the Middle East.
Primitive but very effective. He draped a handkerchief over
the circled thumb and forefinger of his left hand. Like a
magician he poked the cloth into the hole made by the thumb
and forefinger. Doling two or three tablespoons of refined
resin into the cloth sack thus created he would then twist the
bag, and twist, and twist, he would then open the little bag and
turn the ball shaped result upside down and twist again. Bit
by bit the resin would compress and the ball would get
smaller and smaller. It was slow but worked just fine.

Paco was ready to do a production run. He buried his equipment and waited.

Also, they had acquired a dog. They had found it curled up under a bush while out riding south of town in the jungle. It was a thoroughbred German Shepherd and had been shot. Its backbone had been creased leaving a permanent conspicuous dent in mid back. It nevertheless recovered fully. When Paco and Maya went out riding the shepherd would trot behind and savagely chase off any other dogs that would come up from behind to harass the horses. At a full cantor with the shepherd trotting behind they made a pretty picture riding down to the beach for a ride along the beach at sunset. They fed it well so it was the second toughest dog in town (after Steve McQueen's weimeraner who must have eaten steak.) The dogs name was Raven and he hated Mexicans, uniforms, and guns. Paco concluded that he had been shot by a uniformed Mexican.

One day in July they parked the olds on a dusty side street near Jungle Jim's house. They took a cab to their new house with their accumulated stuff. It was a good time to be moving. There were rumors from the Beach boys that their was an 18 man team of Federalies in town that were there to "clean up the drugs". Headed by a motivated former police chief from Guadalajara they were Mexico's best and brightest Law enforcement Officers.

The Mexicans didn't know what was going on but they knew that something was up.

One sign that trouble was in the wind was when Tom Newman packed and left. He had an uncanny instinct for not being there when the shit came down.

They raided the Wheels House. Actually Jungle Jims beach house but Jim had rented it to the Wheel. They found a Listerine bottle sized package that had arrived from Europe and contained 500 doses of Sandoz LSD. They missed an ounce of Hash that Paco had given the Wheel as a down payment for the half Arab horse Talisman. They did find about an ounce of Michoacan seedless pot. (The Wheel only bought the best). Staying at the house had been a small guy called "the Troll" who did odd jobs and deliveries for Tom Newman. He was arrested along with the Wheel. While searching the house the searchers left a guard outside the front door. They had the Wheel upstairs with them and were searching the bedroom. The Troll was handcuffed and left alone in the living room for a few minutes. He saw on the big table that the searching police had set down the Sandoz package and the pot. Backing up to the table the troll opened the container from Sandoz, and removed the vitamin pill size vial from the center of the voluminous packing material. He slipped it where the sun doesn't shine.

He was later released later that day as an unimportant player.

Later that afternoon, at the police station, surrounded by the Jefe and his 6 top hands, the Wheel really displayed his diplomatic skills. The Wheel was an amazing person. Speaking better Spanish than most of his interrogators he protested, "gentlemen gentlemen, it is so uncomfortable on a hot day to be crowded into this little room. There is a lovely restaurant across the street from Police Headquarters. Why don't we all have lunch and you can ask me all the questions you want to. I'm eager to cooperate. I will pay for lunch of course. I realize that you are not paid much. It will be "my treat".

"Well, all right" the Jefe said trying to be very stern as his position required. He warned the Wheel "don't get any funny ideas". "Of course not" said the Wheel.

His men hadn't eaten since early in the day and it was almost time for the main meal of the day. While the Jefe and six of his troops packed away dinner. The Wheel kept them so enthralled with stories from the history of their own country, that they hardly said a word and forgot to ask any questions. After dinner the Wheel said "cabelleros since we are all real men I am sure that you, like me, would like to go get laid after a nice meal like this". There was a murmur of obligatory assent. "Well heck guys I know a great cathouse just a little ways up the coast, in Guerrero. We could be there in an hour. What do you say it will be my treat. They have some beautiful girls, with dark eyes and long hair, and you can interrogate me while we have a little fun. Life is short".   After a quick huddle the Jefe and his crew said "OK but don't get any funny ideas".

"Of course not" said the Wheel.

This process continued for a week. Restaurant by Restaurant, Town by town, Charming Hotel by Charming Hotel, Cathouse by Cathouse they wined and dined their way towards the border. The Wheel knew the West Coast of Mexico like the back of his hand. Finally arriving at the border the Jefe escorted him to the US entry point and wrung his hand. Brushing a tear from his eye he pumped the hand of the Wheel.

"Ohhh thank you senor, thank you" he said, "that was the best time any of us have ever had. If you ever come back to our country please give me a call here is my card."

Meanwhile back in PV, the other twelve Federals were getting a line on Paco. They didn't know what he was doing with it but they knew he was buying Kilos of Pot. It turned out that the old man who supplied Paco was telling them how much Paco had been buying. They assumed he was smuggling it out but couldn't figure out how. They kept watch on the beaches and tried to figure out what was going on.

Paco and Maya were very happy there but they knew about the Federals. Their visas were expired and it was time to go. But a couple hundred dollars would barely get them to the border and they would need money when they got there. They were invited to Hollywood and had been offered the lofty social title of "Hashmaker to the Stars". It sounded like fun but they would need some hash. They would have to make it right under the noses of the 18 man federal team.

They lived very normal lives. They engaged in very little social activity and kept to themselves at the north end of town.

They saw the Federals around town and the beach. They developed nicknames for some of them. The tall one, the short one, the crewcut, the pig. They didn't seem to be watching the new house. There wasn't much to watch.

Their new house on the north end of town was up on the hill above the electric plant, near where "Café des Artistes" is now. The summer rate was about 50 bucks a month and they paid two months ahead. Paco removed some bricks from the floor of the guest house and buried his hash making tools and small stash.

The pace was still very laid back. A fisherman would knock on their door and Maya would select a "watchanongo" (red snapper) from several hanging on an oar. They brought their groceries up one afternoon a week when Paco would rent a burro to carry them up the steep hill. They would cook dishes from the "Gourmet cookbook". They would eat stuffed Snapper and Soufle while they watched the dolphins jump in the moonlight in the bay. They took siestas in the afternoon when it rained. Some times they would ride on the beach at sunset. With the Wheel gone, Maya had the use of the Arabian Horse "Talisman" She would ride it into the water, and gallop along the hard sand by the waters edge. She was a vision of wild and free, healthy and beautiful.

For recreation and to lull the watchers they spent their spare time (what was left after lovemaking and cooking) in making chess sets out of clay and painting them. Castles for rooks, nights on flying pterodactyls mounted on pedestals. Hooded monks for bishops, The Queen had a long blue gown, a crown and a needle for a wand. The King was crosslegged on a toadstool and smoked a pipe.

Paco went over to Jungle Jim's house for their weekly chess game. Jim knew about the Federals but wasn't bothered. He was married to a upper-class solvent Mexican woman from a good family who was above reproach. Occasionally one of the Federals would climb a palm tree across the street when Paco was there for chess. Jim would go into the house and come back with a Walthers automatic pistol and point it at the climber. They would climb down. Back then you could still do things like that if you were a property owner.

Paco wanted to borrow the gun. He had decided to go into the hills to contact the old man.

It's dangerous in there said Jim, there's Indians and bandits. Also there were animals, jaguars, and wolves for example, not to mention snakes.

He had a point with the snakes, thought Paco who had recently been swimming near the river mouth and had encountered several. He hadn't known that the rains washed them down from the hills in the flash floods of the rainy season. One snake had reared on the surface of the water and attacked. Paco dove deep. He came up and realized that he was surrounded by various land snakes swimming near the river mouth. Edging away toward shore he was startled by pelicans diving all around him as they came in for the food. The flock of pelicans crashed into the water from thirty and forty feet up all around and within inches of Paco. A week later the Mexicans shot the pelicans for interfering with the fishing. They also shot all the stray dogs every year too.

Jim lent Paco the Pistol and recommended a jeep rental place on the Malecon. You should take a jeep and a guide, he said. It would take days on horseback.

Paco rented a Jeep from a tourist place that rented by the day. It was 15 or 20 dollars and was intended for use driving around town to look good for the girls.

As he was leaving a tall Mexican walked up to the side of the jeep and asked if he was going into the interior and if so could he get a lift. He said he wanted to visit family who lived up there. He offered to pay. Paco had to make a quick decision. "Well I need a guide thought Paco and it would bring the cost of the Jeep rental down' so he said "sure 100 peso's". Paco assumed it was a cop. It was a pretty safe assumption under the circumstances. "Well, thought Paco, I'm not holding anything, and after I drop this guy off where he pretends he's going I will be near the old mans village. They already know

I'm going. Paco didn't think that they knew exactly where or who he was going to see. He thought, "after all the Wheel does this stuff all the time. Shove come to push I'm armed and he's not". It's an ironclad rule never to travel alone in Mexico but he didn't want to subject Maya to any danger after the Marscota trip. "Ok, hope he knows the way."

Paco and his "guide" headed into the hills.

It was the rainy season so we are not really talking about roads here. Wash out, three-foot deep potholes, water above the hood constantly. Jim had been right this would have been very difficult on horseback. At first as they approached the foothills it wasn't bad but the water was a killer. 15 times they had to stop and remove the distributor cap and dry the points. The muffler and air intake were upright so the Jeep could go with the engine under water but the points kept getting wet. They were constantly in 4-wheel low rocking over the ruts and boulders. The Olds wouldn't have made the first ten miles. Late in the afternoon they arrived at the edge of the Americas River. It had been Paco's original plan to reach the village above the river where they had loaded the Olds on the cattle truck, and then as he came back to stop in the village of the old man and order some pot. He was looking for about 15 Kilos. More if he could score cheaper further into the hills but the probable cop in the passenger ruled that out. The guy was a little too well dressed for the wild country. Paco pegged him as a city guy.

The Jefe of the Federalies and 10 or more of his team were waiting by the edge of the wide deeper than the Jeep river. They pretended to be a federal posse. They all had riding stuff on but they had four-wheel drive tucks nearby.

They were very courteous. "Where are you going senor?" "Up to the big village above the river" said Paco "I want to go hunting." This had been Paco's "cover story" since he had left PV.

They talked among themselves and said "but of course we must help you" and with huge grins they had lifted the Jeep across the deepest part of the river in water up their wastes laughing and joking about Paco's story about going hunting with the 9mm Walthers. Paco realized two things. One was that they didn't know what he was doing but they had to help him do it or they would have nothing to bust him for. Two the Jeep would never make it back across the river. It was too valuable in the interior. Because of the extortionate import duties some rancher would pay 5 times its retail US value for it. The Jefe knew this and was pleased to help the "tourist hunter" further out onto a limb so to speak. Even if he didn't find out where the gringo was buying his pot at least he would wind up with the Jeep to sell.

Paco would have turned around and headed back but he had to stick to his cover story.

Late that night around 11 o'clock the distributor rotor was being dried for the 100th time and as it was being replaced, it broke. Paco couldn't remember if he did it or the "guide" but the Jeep was down. Paco decided to head back. "Aren't you coming?" he said to the "guide"? "No I will stay with the Jeep and guard it". "Sure you will" thought Paco and wondered how long it would take the "posse" to catch up and find a distributor rotor. He caught a ride with a tractor whose owner didn't believe he was up there hunting either. And then a truck, which got him back across the river. He had to walk the last 15 miles slogging down the road out of the foot hills wading through the basins washouts and water filled pot holes two and three feet deep. It was around 4 AM and dark but there was a little starlight. As he slogged along mile after mile Paco could make out shapes. He was on a long straight stretch with only water filled ruts for obstacles. He was wearing low boots (snakes) but they were full of water and had been for miles. The gun hung down from the front of his pants and was heavy.

He heard the Wolves before he sensed their movement. He was walking past a little ranch with a shuttered and sealed one room house. What looked like a pack of dogs was sniffing around the outside. He could see the movement and hear the sounds but not any detail except the outline of the small house that looked like it was made out of sticks. They spotted Paco and headed over. There was about 5 of them. Paco had time to pull the pistol as they ducked under the rail fence and surrounded him. Paco slide the slide back and thought he had chambered a round. He clicked off the safety as the Alpha animal came closer and closer snarling.

Paco had read that the alpha of the hunting group always leads the attack so although he could sense the others circling beside and behind him Paco focused on the snarling animal in front of him. The alpha Wolves teeth were bared and it was perhaps an inch from the muzzle of the Walther. Paco pulled the trigger.

The gun didn't fire. For a moment there was a total silence. The sound of the hammer falling on the empty chamber was loud in the dark and the alpha wolf was instantly silent, sniffing the barrel of the pistol. Paco never thought to re-chamber a round. He was paralyzed be the image of being buried under a pile of fur and teeth. Before he could think of why the gun hadn't fired the wolf finished its inspection of the gun barrel and whirled away taking its four companions off up the road into the night.

As he slogged along he thought the only thing that hasn't happened is a venomous snake and a Jaguar. He saw the drowned body of a very small rattlesnake further on as the sun rose but no his relief no Jaguars. He came out of the valley by the airport and walked back to the house. He reported the Jeep missing and the owner rushed off into the hills to look for it.

The next afternoon Paco was walking along the beach at Los Muertos in the Old Town. He was planning to return the pistol to Jungle Jim at his beach house.

He passed the various beach restaurants that catered to the tourists. As he passed one shaded restaurant people seemed to rise out the sand. He was suddenly surrounded. They were so raggedy they were obviously local PV Police. They were pissed. First of all the Jeep was history. The Federals had stolen it and the locals got nothing and it was all the fault of this gringo who was carrying a gun down their beach (under his shirt but they weren't that stupid.) The ring around him started to close slowly. They were afraid he would fight or flee and after all he was armed so they were careful to move in such a way that they would block all escape routes.

At that moment something very beautiful happened.

Maya saved his ass.

Did she ever.

She was too much and a half and then some.

It was a stupendous thing to do.

It was right on a par with the time he had built the road and changed the wheels underwater to get them out of the fast deep river by the cliff below Marscota.

He would love her forever for it.

A horse broke through the circle and reared up flailing its hooves. It was a beautiful powerful black Arabian animal with a head like a chiseled chess piece. It was Talisman. In the saddle was Maya.

The men around Paco fell back as Talisman continued to rear and flail. Maya controlled him with a perfect touch and kept him standing on his rear two legs. Leaning forward in the saddle to compensate for the standing flailing horse she called out in her perfect Castilian Spanish in a voice like an excited child "Paco, Paco, I have just come from the telegraph office. My rich father in New York has sent me a lot of money Paco. A lot of money. We will never be poor here again". She let Talisman come back onto all fours and walked him around Paco talking seriously as she went on still in Spanish. "Really a lot of money Paco", she said, "many thousands of dollars". Then her usually musical voice took on a hard cutting edge as she turned from him to look around the circle of raggedy cops. "More than enough to buy the lives of all these she said with a disdainful all-inclusive gesture of her hand."

The local cops turned away and left.

Maya had been riding further down the beach and had been keeping an eye on him.

The next day there was a knock on the door. It was the old man (and his burro) I heard you were in the hills looking for me he said.

THE CHASE

A few days later around 9 in the evening a large sack come over the garden wall. It was about 12 kilos of good pot. It cost about $180.00 US.

The Federal Team rewarded the Old man for his information with his own khaki uniform, Sam Brown belt, and a shiny badge. He was now "one of them" and in charge of drug enforcement in the little village below the river but outside of town.

Paco didn't know any of that at the time but he assumed from the stepped up surveillance that they knew he had scored. He also figured that they would wait for him to actually try to smuggle it before they would pounce.

The problem for the Federals was they didn't have a clue that he was processing the pot into Hash. They had never encountered hash and it didn't occur to them. Paco knew they were waiting for him to move with what they knew had to be at least a suitcase full of Pot.

Paco and Maya closed the shutters and working late at night cleaned and stripped the buds and leaves from the stems and separated out the seeds. It took a few days but they slowly reduced the bulk. Twice Paco rode bareback down to the beach at dusk on Talisman wearing sandals and long baggy gym pants. He would ride into the surf and reaching down in the gathering darkness he would untie the bottoms of the pants and let the seeds and chopped stems flow out into the sea.

After extracting nearly a pound of resin Paco and Maya were left with about 7 or eight pounds of chopped leaf containing the residue from the extraction process. It was of various grades of quality and concentration. Some of the best he gave to Jungle Jim to have for a general supply. The rest he divided into half-pound lots and sold them in bulk to the Beach boys who had been his eyes and ears. They were delighted to get the resin extracted but still quite decent pot all cleaned chopped and ready to sell to the tourists. They jumped at the chance to pay about 2/3rds of the going rate and paid cash in Peso's. This helped the getaway fund greatly. They also sold the trusty Oldsmobile that hadn't run for months and no mechanic could fix it. The got $45.00 US for it.

The various Federals would watch them but still hadn't a clue what they were actually doing. They were especially puzzled by what Paco did for the next week or so. One of them reported back "I don't know Jefe we have 6 men watching at a time changing shifts every eight hours. But all he does is sit on the breach and twist that rag. He must have a nervous problem Jefe he is always twisting that rag". "Maybe he is frightened of us", said the Jefe. "Don't let him out of your sight. When he goes to take all that pot up north we going to get him for sure".

Paco went to the beach every day for two weeks and sat in a chair looking out to sea and twisting a rag in his hand as though it was some sort of nervous habit. He was making classic "Hash Balls". There were 16 of them at about an ounce each.

They finally finished processing the "batch" and disposed of the tools, materials, and residue into the sea. Putting the 16 golf ball size ounces into a small cloth bag. They prepared to leave.

It wasn't as easy as you might think. First of all they had the dog, second after 8 months "in the interior" even though they lived in a nice house they were pretty aculturated.
Talisman would stay at his stable where Jungle Jim would look after him. With their luggage, large dog, various baskets and clothes, food to travel with and the guitar they were pretty encumbered. Followed closely by the Federals they took a cab to the airport and took a $5.00 each flight to Tepic where there was a railway headed north.

On the way to the airport the mechanic that he had sold the car to (getting a receipt from Mr. Hokum Lutchmuck that the car was sold for parts.) passed with the Olds running perfectly and now in use as a taxi. Aiiiiiiieeeeeee Grinnngo the driver yelled as he passed them at about 60 miles an hour.

The aircraft was a single engine piper that made the run twice a week. They squeezed in along with a large lady with a suitcase several baskets and 2 chickens, I swear, two chickens. What with Paco and Maya, the dog and the pilot it was a very crowded Piper Cub.

Their ears popped and the aircraft struggled like a motor scooter in low gear to get over the mountains but landed safely in Tepic less than an hour later. They were on their way.

They bought tickets on the train to Nogales, which was a border town across from New Mexico. They were told "Senor, you cannot take the dog on the train." "Sure" said Paco.

They got on the train and settled into seats with the dog at their feet as the train pulled out and started to rattle across the great northern desert. Two of the Federals sat a couple seats ahead and two sat a couple seats behind. Pretty soon the conductor came by for their tickets and said "Senor you cannot have the dog on the train". "He's not leaving" said Paco. The conductor went and got the chief conductor. All this took time so they had been traveling about an hour when the chief conductor bustled up and said "Senor you cannot have this dog on the train it is forbidden". "Oh yeah" said Paco "this dog is staying". And he tied the dog's leash to the seat. "There" said Paco "now whadaya gonna do." The conductor came back after about an hour with four soldiers armed with rifles and an officer. The train stopped near some godforsaken little pueblo, and Paco, Maya, the dog Raven, and their luggage were removed from the train at gunpoint. .

Standing by the tracks Paco heard the officer give the order "shoot the dog". "Wait" Paco said, and he pleaded for the dog's life. " We will get a crate and take another train with the dog as baggage", he said. Finally he threatened the officer. "I have come to this country for many years. I always come back. When I come back I always remember my friends. I also remember those who have done ill to me. There will be a record somewhere of what officer was on this train this day and if you shoot my dog I will be back to see you again someday.".

The officer paused, He ordered the soldier who was about to shoot the dog to search Paco. The soldier did. It was a young kid who was distracted by Maya. Paco had the bag of Hash balls tied behind his crotch. As he was searched the kid's hand hefted the sack and his eyes grew a little wide but he continued on. "He is clean" said the kid. The officer and his troops got back on the train, which then pulled out.

There was only one small 2-story hotel in the little town where the train had stopped.

There was only one other guest. It was an American who said he was a prospector. It was obviously to Paco that this was a U.S. Federal Cop. The guy with the crewcut and polished shoes claimed he was in the area looking for opals. 'Yeah thought Paco and I'm a Jaguar hunter with a 9mm automatic'.

The guy went on and on with his story trying to become friendly and kept making inquiries about where they were going. Paco made the sign to Maya which meant "keep this turkey distracted" bringing his finger from his eye he moved it first toward her and then toward the overweight obvious plant who was going on about his shoes being too tight.

Paco went outside on some pretext, scaled the outside of the building and entered the guys room through the balcony. There was no evidence of opal prospecting equipment, no rock hammers no sample bags, zip. Just a brand new paperback on gemstones that had barely been opened. Paco went back down the outside of the building and returning to the lobby he touched Maya's shoulder with a quick triple tap. It was a prearranged signal and it meant, "I'm up tight lets split". They made their excuses and went upstairs to their own room.

Talking in their own language, using signs for key words, Maya and he reached the following conclusions:

The anti drug agencies of both countries were involved.

The US was already tipped off he was coming

They were really overt and clumsy.

They were looking for a large suitcase full of pot.

They didn't know anything about the Hash.

They had been kicked off the train at that town on purpose so they could run into this American Fed.

The fed was supposed to find out where they were going. Also if they had the pot with them.

Paco wondered if they thought he had it or had somehow passed the "suitcase full of pot" to a confederate and was planning to take possession just below the border and attempt to get it across. It made sense. It's how they thought. Raven guarded their luggage like it was full of steak.

They went down to dinner and made nice to the "Prospector".

Paco examined him about opals and mining. He was reminded of Oswald LeWinter when the guy tried to make up answers. They didn't challenge him however. On the contrary Paco expressed sincere concern for the guy's sore feet and gave him his own sandals. I will be wearing shoes up north said Paco and you really need them. They are your size and are really great sandals. He insisted and the relived cop took them.

Paco figured that their luggage would be gone through at some point but never left it unguarded in an effort to convince the watchers that he might just have it with him.

The next morning the "Opal Prospector" seemed a little bewildered as they got back on another train after tying the dog in the baggage compartment with food and water. Take care of those feet called Paco from the open window as the train pulled out.

The 18-man team was back. They changed every few hours and were predictable and recognizable after months being around PV. They sat a few seats away at all times. Around noon the train had stopped at some totally godforsaken water hole in the middle of the desert to add water to the steam engine boiler.

The train was just pulling out when Paco looked out the window and saw Raven trotting around the squalid collection of shacks. Tail high and gate easy there was no doubt it was he.

The train was gathering speed Paco jumped up. "Ya mi voy" (I am going) he said in a loud voice to Maya and went to the end of the car to pull the emergency chord. By the time he pulled it the train had gone miles and would go several miles more before it slowly ground to a stop.

The conductors had come running and Paco had demanded they stop the train,which was still rocketing through the desert. The conductors gave in and pulled the cord in a series of signals that told the engineer to stop the train.

Paco issued instructions while the train slowly slowed down with much squealing and grinding. He was going to go back on foot. He ordered the conductor to stop the train at the next town however small, and leave Maya there. Maya was to stay put and Paco would be there somehow. If possible she should send horses back get him. There were no roads or cars just the track cutting through the desolate alkali desert brush. The conductor agreed to make an unscheduled stop at the next little pueblo 20 miles up the line to allow Maya to get off.

Paco got off the train and watched it disappear into the distance headed north. He was concerned. He didn't know when he would see Maya again. With her excellent Spanish he was sure she could cope but he was concerned.

He started south along the track. It was about 7 or 8 miles before he saw the water tower in the distance and shortly after entered the motley collection of shacks and old boxcars that were being used for houses. He got a drink from the well and as he helped a woman draw a heavy bucket he heard snarling and barking. "That's Raven" thought Paco and moments later Raven was released from where some wretch had tied him up and they were together again. Raven seemed inordinately proud of his exploit and pranced around like he was on parade with Talisman and the Palomino. "I'll bet it was a Mexican in uniform that you attacked on the train and that's why you got thrown off" thought Paco.

Starting north again they covered mile after mile. It was very surreal. They passed many waterholes that were poisoned. The dead animals surrounding them that had drunk the water were numerous and odiferous. The heat, the sun, the corpses, the wavering air above the tracks shimmered as the afternoon passed. In the late afternoon Paco saw shapes emerging out of the shimmering heat waves above the track to the north. It was horses. It was rescue. Maya had sent them. What a woman. She was the greatest woman Paco had ever known. Dear God how he loved her.

She had sent two men on horseback with an extra horse to get
him. They had brought water, and a bag of oranges. It was
about 10 more miles to the little village.   Mexicans have a
great natural sense of drama. And as they drew close to the
village they broke into a cantor and with Raven prancing and
strutting and savagely defending the rear of the horses from
the handful of malnourished local mongrels. It was a grand
entrance. Maya was sitting cross-legged in the center of a
dusty circle near a bare 4 foot by 40 foot concrete pad that
was where the train had stopped to let her off. The conductor
had wanted to go further but she had insisted so they had
stooped and let her off. She was surrounded be the entire
male population of the village, maybe thirty guys. Every one
of them was firing pistols into the air in celebration of the
"rescue". Many thought he was crazy for going so far in that
desert for a dog but others admired the exploit. One man was
obviously the Jefe and carried a stick about the size of a cane.
Paco knew he was the headman because of the stick. It just fit.

"That was a great thing" the headman said, "to go to so much trouble to rescue a dog". Paco was pleased by the reception but it was almost dark and he wanted to get going. "How can we get to the road" he asked, "we need to get to the next city on the rail line so we can get back on the next train but first we have to get to a paved road".

Many of the men were very eager to help, a little too eager, they quickly produced a battered four-wheel drive farm truck and said let's go. It seemed like every male in the village wanted to go along. They were so bright eyed and eager. He was about to climb up when the headman caught his eye and made the left right sign with his eyes. It meant watch out. He invited Paco to be his guest for the night and to take the flat bed truck/bus with wooden benches that came through in the morning and could take them to a Highway where they could catch a bus for the next city where the train stopped.
Paco was reluctant but when the Jefe called his attention to the eager faces on the truck it dawned on that they looked exactly like the yahoos from Texas.

The headman insisted and sternly admonished Maya. "If you had not sat all afternoon cross-legged they would not be like this he said. A good woman sits on the ground with her legs together and her knees drawn up", he explained. They sat around a fire by the headman's tiny shack and ate simple food. Some of the villagers came by and reheard the story of the dog and the rescue. Others told stories of the bush. Several dozen scorpions had hit one guy when he had fallen from his horse into a bush, but they were the black kind and only had the effect of bad bee stings. The Headman told Paco and Maya about huge caves full of bat guano in the mountains above the rail line. Paco filed the information away for future exploitation. Paco and Maya washed in buckets of rainwater, slept in hammocks outdoors under the lean-to roof, and the Jefe stood guard over them all night with a 22 rifle. They found out at some point that during the entire afternoon Maya had sat by the tracks not one of the entire town's males had told any of the women in town that she was there.

In the morning a flat bed farm truck lurched through with wooden benches bolted to the bed. For small change they got a lurching rocking ride for about 20 miles out to where the dusty trail met the highway.

They made their way to the train and this time had a wire crate made up and started out again. Headed North. They had obviously shaken their tail when they got off the train but as soon as they were settled in their seats they were right there. This is getting monotonous. They really didn't have a plan as they got closer to the border. Then fate stepped in and helped them make one About two in the afternoon of the next day about a hundred miles below the border in a huge train-switching yard the train stopped That's all there was to the town was a huge train yard.

There was to be a 7-hour layover the conductor said then a different train would go the rest of the way to the border. They got Raven from the baggage car and their luggage.

After crossing several tracks they came to a low shed like building that rented rooms to the layover passengers for a couple of dollars. Paco had noticed the afternoon shift

Federal guys looked pretty tired. It was a hot sleepy afternoon. Paco yawned and stretched guess its time for a Siesta he said in loud voice. They checked in and so did the Federals. There was not a sound outside any of the little rooms. They all opened onto a shed walkway that led to the one shower and toilet.

1st Paco and Maya repacked and consolidated. They were wide-awake and fully alert but absolutely silent, communicating only in signs. They got rid of the baskets and travel food under their bed. Each room had one dusty window out the back. Paco opened it and saw a little used path behind the building. He waited until he was sure their tail was asleep. They had seemed very tired and after all where could their quarry go?

Next, Paco reconnoitered. In the bathroom above the shower was a false ceiling. Old and tattered it was really a woven mat but it lowered the height of the ceiling a couple feet. Paco was looking for a place to dump the stash where he could come back for it. It looked like no one had looked up there for years. It was dusty but dry. Paco put the sack of hash balls up there and covered it with a little dusty scrap of mat so even if you stood on a chair and looked you wouldn't see it in the dark corner. Should be ok thought Paco. He had a great sense of relief as he came back from his shower to take his "Siesta". He no longer could be busted for the 12 kilos. or for the processed hash. He didn't have it. He did have one small half-marble sized piece, which he put in his pocket.

Then while the world around him slept through the "Siesta" on the sleepy hot summer afternoon Paco went out the rear window and found the local bus station that existed for the train workers and their families. "Yes there was a 3rd class bus for the border leaving at 5:00 PM. It was a three-hour ride." Paco bought 2 tickets. Coming back behind the little hostel he reentered through the rear window.

They waited until 4:45. Maya went out the back window first and Paco handed out the two bags and the dog. Then he came out with his guitar. They made it to the bus station as the bus was loading. Paco tied Raven underneath in the luggage compartment. They got on and got seats near the rear. The bus pulled out.

They watched the cactus and foothills roll by as they made their way to the border. They were surprised their were no checkpoints but it later turned out that access to the train yard town was for Mexicans only and was off limits to tourists, therefore no checkpoints.

They got off the bus at the Nogales bus station and walked across into the US. At the last moment as they approached the border Paco put the half marble into his nose. He gave an extra push and it disappeared into his sinus cavity. They walked across with the evening foot traffic with their bags and dog.

"Where are you from" they were asked.

"Boston" said Paco

"New York" said Maya.

That was it they were in. They were back in the U S of A.
Paco had a stuffy nose, and their stash was 100 miles below
the border.

BACK IN THE USA

Their first priority after crossing was to get away from the border area and be sure that the ordeal of surveillance was over.

They tried to get a bus to Taos but could not get on a US bus with the dog.

"Not allowed said the driver".

"How about underneath" said Paco.

"Not allowed" said the driver.

They hitchhiked to Taos New Mexico. It was a hard hitch. They had too much stuff plus the large dog.

They were sitting by the side of the road in their really outlandish (for the US) attire. They had really become very acculturated. They looked like the gypsies they were. Paco had a wide mustache, a straw hat and a deep dark tan. Maya was dark and exotic with sun-bleached hair under a straw sunhat. She was wearing one of her "Mexican Peasant Girl fashion creations". They were simple and comfortable.

They were both tired and hot when a local trooper pulled up and demanded ID.

Since they had thrown the Lutchmuck paperwork and their two-month expired Mexican visas in a trash can immediately upon reentry they dug into their packs and produced their well-stamped passports. Paco's had several pages of Arabic and Spanish stamps and was well worn but valid.

Looking from the photos in the passports at the two brown individuals with the shaded hats the trooper squinted and said, "Well if you is American Citizens, how come you is carrying Passports?". He said it with the air of a trial attorney making a damning point.

Maya was pretty tired, she wearily looked up and said

"Well Officer, exactly what document do you suggest that we carry to prove our citizenship."

It would have made a great cartoon for the "New Yorker".

The troopers Adam's apple went up and down for a while and he handed back their documents "Ah guess yew got a point thar" he allowed, and took off. Paco and Maya laughed for twenty minutes. Each of them replayed the scene mimicking the officer and Maya.

Not long later an old car slowly come along driven by an old man. He approached going 20 miles an hour. He had room for them all and continued at 20 miles an hour. They rode for a day with ""Pop". Who was in no hurry. He had no papers no registration no license.

 Paco was amazed. "Don't you get pulled over?"

"Sure" the old man said but if they put me in jail I just rest up then gets going again." It was a fun ride. The old guy was a character and after all the stress of the trip up they were glad to slow the pace. Eventually he left them off not too far from Taos and they made it in.

They rented a room for a couple days. Paco had been feeling strange and fell into a deep sleep. Maya was worried. When he woke up after several hours his nose was packed and starting to swell. He felt pretty good but knew the hash had to come out. By blowing his nose into a towel the half marble of great hash emerged more or less intact.

They had a pipe and some great sex and thus refreshed checked out the area. They were obviously of no interest to anybody and it felt good to be anonymous. They had cleaned up and looked a little more normal more or less. They took long walks with the dog on the Indian Reservation near by and could see they were alone.

The first thing they had to address was how to travel. Hitching was a no go. It was difficult and dangerous. Paco didn't have enough money to buy a car although that wasn't out of the question. Paco still had a spare driver's license under the name G. W. Hiccup. They really wanted to get a bus to LA.

They also wanted their stash.

They were walking past a leather goods store that made and sold all sorts of luggage. "We make anything" the sign said.

So Paco had a Seeing Eye dog harness made for Raven. They had to approximate some things but a basic large size dog harness with three luggage handles attached looked pretty close. Paco put on wraparound dark glasses and practiced walking with him on a couple back streets of Taos. Raven thought it was a new game and responded to signal clicks that Paco would make. Stopping and starting, turning left and right on cue.

"It'll work," he said.

Paco shaved off his moustache. They packed up and took a bus back to the border. No one said a word about the dog as they got on the bus and rode through the night. The dog stayed quiet and they caught some sleep. Paco stared out at the world from behind his dark glasses.

Arriving at the border town in the morning they rented a cheap room. Paco put a suit, tie, and dress shoes into a paper bag. They took a walk toward the border crossing point with Maya carrying a paper bag and leading hunched over Paco the blind man with his Seeing Eye dog. As they passed an alley Paco stepped in. Taking off his clothes and putting them in the bag he removed the suit, tie, and shoes. He quickly changed clothes. It was a dramatic change.

From the scruffy hunched over blind man he was instantly transformed into the tall American businessman Mr. G. W. Hiccup. He left the dog with Maya who undid the harness and put Raven on a leash. She exited the alley from the way they had come in.

Exiting at the opposite end of the alley the tall American "businessman" walked directly to the exit point from the US. Striding purposefully across the border G.W. Hiccup walked up to Mexican Immigration and demanded to speak to someone. To the official who responded he requested permission to go to the train yard town. '

"Senor it is not allowed for tourists", he was told.

"I'm not a tourist" thundered GW in pretty good Spanish, "I have to go see my forwarding agent Senor Enrique Gonzalez. I have crates of import goods coming in by train they must be handled by a Mexican forwarding agent in that town".

The official couldn't follow quite what he was saying but shrugged and issued a 14-day visa for Mr. G. W. Hiccup to go to the town of the rail yard.

Paco took the 11:AM bus. It got in around 2 PM. He checked in at the layover place and went to the shower.

It was still there.

He waited in his room until 4:45, then went out the back window and caught the 5:PM bus back up. Around 8:30 PM he walked across the border. G. W. Hiccup was back from his day's business. He was not challenged.

Not many minutes later and a few blocks from the border Mr. G. W. entered one end of the same alley he had left from in the morning. Out the other end came the wretched blind man with the Seeing Eye dog and the pretty gypsy girl guiding him and carrying a paper bag.

They went back to their room and had another pipe of the half marble. They made love.

Several times.

In the morning they took the bus for LA.

The bus ride to LA didn't go so well. Welll that's an understatement.

The good news was that they got there.

The bad news was that everything that could go wrong did.

Raven took off after several other dogs hanging around the Bus Station. A bitch in Heat caught his attention and he frantically pulled to get at her. He fought with two other male dogs and lunged barking and snarling at three uniformed policeman. He growled and snapped at the bus driver who also wore a uniform and worse yet for him was Mexican.

In between battles Raven was restless and friendly and wanted to "work the room" for handouts. It was a charming but bad habit that he had picked up on the beaches.

Some people, can you believe it, some people actually thought Paco might not be really blind. A certain level of hostility built up. Paco stared out the window and moved his head like a robot. It wasn't the best blind man imitation ever done. At the rest stop after struggling with his food he finally gave up and just ate it.

At the rest stop Raven got in two more fights with other dogs. He snarled at the bus driver, again. It was a real dog and pony show. They looked like a traveling circus act. They were uniquely conspicuous. It was comical from one viewpoint but nerve wracking from another.

Arriving in LA it was late so they put in a call to Barryless on a pay phone and checked into a hotel. Paco had to keep his mouth shut when the bellboy deliberately shortchanged him. Flatly denying the denomination of the bill, saying a five was a one. What could Paco say. After all he was blind, wasn't he?

They cleaned up and got some sleep.

In the morning they called Barryless again and this time got through to the housekeeper who said "that Barryless was expecting them but was "on location" and wouldn't be available until 4: PM."

"4:00 PM that's not bad" thought Paco "we'll check out at noon and take a walk down sunset strip. We can Call JB from Hollywood and walk there from down town or take a bus".

It was too far to walk with their baggage so they took a bus. The blind man thing worked so they were able to take a LA city bus out to Sunset Boulevard at about the 8500 block, about a mile from Beverly Hills.

They were near Laurel Canyon when they got of the bus. It was hot and they slowly started to walk along Sunset Boulevard carrying their bags with the dog still in the harness.

They had seen a policeman on the bus that looked like a LA detective well dressed and intent. They noticed some one was slowly walking a block behind them keeping pace also well dressed and intent. They looked ahead of them and in side a glass doorway someone was watching them over the top of a newspaper also well dressed and intent.

It was the La Bunco squad and they were triangulated.

"They probably thought they were trying to run a Seeing Eye dog gypsy scam of some sort" thought Paco as he realized they didn't have long if they were that close.

"This is an unexpected problem", thought Paco, "if they roust us or bust us they will find the hash". They were definitely closing in.

Heaven opened her gates one more time for these two souls who really had been through a long tough journey fun though it might have been.

A long Lincoln Limousine swept up to the curb. The door swung open.

It was Harry and Larry, their neighbors from Puerto Vallarta.

Squeals of delight, shrieks of recognition and joy. Friends. They were instantly loaded into the cool velvet interior. The dog, guitar, suitcases, and themselves. The door closed and the blast of the Air Conditioner hit them. It was terrific. The limo pulled away.

Paco looked out the window at the three plainclothes policemen who were all scratching their heads.

Harry and Larry whisked them up to their Hollywood Hills house where they relaxed in luxury while smoking the last of the half marble of hash, told their stories, and unpacked the stash.

Around 4:30 Barryless came and got them and they were off to the Beach House in Malibu. They were now entering an entirely different world. They were off to be wined, dined and honored as "Hashmakers to the Stars".

They later found out that male dogs are never used as Seeing Eye dogs which is probably what got the "Bunco squad" on their tail.

They bought an old Cadillac and didn't need to take buses any more so Raven was returned to normal dog status. He still hated police and guns.

I wish I could say that they lived happily ever after but that's another story

www.ingramcontent.com/pod-product-compliance
Lightning Source LLC
Chambersburg PA
CBHW070843300326
41935CB00039B/1383